What People Are Saying
Raising Children on Pu

D1360513

Raising Children on Purpose is very easy to read and extremely practical. At a time when people have so many activities on their plate, it brings into focus the need to purposely evaluate and structure a program for the development of our children. The mere fact that it causes one to spend time reflecting on how they can be more effective parents makes this an absolutely invaluable tool. I hope it will prove beneficial to many generations of young parents.

—*Benjamin S. Carson, Sr., M.D.*
Director of Pediatric Neurosurgery
Johns Hopkins

Practical, practical, full of hope!

As a window into children—and a mirror to parents—Wes helps us see and celebrate kids' God-given uniqueness, and these pages hold a powerful, practical tool for every parent who wants to raise children according to God's dream for them. A valuable, anyone-can-do resource for us as parents. Thanks, Wes!

—*Joani Schultz*
Chief Creative Officer
Group Publishing

Wesley Fleming delivers wisdom with such sensitivity and wit that each step of the book makes you eager to try its principles out. I learned wonderful insights for my own role as a parent, but also for how I can grow as a person, as a son reflecting on my own past.

—*Craig Keener*
Professor of New Testament, Palmer Theological Seminary
Author of *The IVP Bible Background Commentary: New Testament*

What People Are Saying about Wesley Fleming's Ministry

As you sit on the edge of your seat, the Scriptures come alive....Wes exhorts men and women to godly living, confronting sensitive issues with humor and insight. The result is life-changing decisions.

—Single father with two sons

Wesley Fleming's presentation provides practical, biblically based insights into parenting. His style is down-to-earth and humorous. The day flew by, and we came away with ideas and techniques we could apply immediately.

—Parents of three preschoolers

Wesley's seminar touched me personally and challenged me as a parent. We have implemented much of what we learned in our home and are seeing exciting results!

—Mother of two teens

RAISING
CHILDREN ON PURPOSE

HELPING YOUR CHILDREN FIND THEIR GOD-GIVEN CALLING

Dedication

To Vicki, my wife and best friend,
my daughters Rebekah, Rachael, Beth,
and the following friends who believed that God
could do a little with a lot, a lot with a little,
and everything with nothing:
Peg, Donald and Margaret, Mark, Louis,
Sue, Anne, and Anna.

RAISING
CHILDREN ON PURPOSE

HELPING YOUR CHILDREN FIND THEIR GOD-GIVEN CALLING

WESLEY H. FLEMING

WHITAKER
HOUSE

Excerpts from *What My Parents Did Right* by Gloria Gaither are reprinted with the permission of Howard Books, a Division of Simon & Schuster Adult Publishing Group. © 2002 Gloria Gaither. Excerpt from "In the Father's Arms," *Preaching Today Audio Series*, tape no. 141, a sermon by Jill Briscoe, is quoted with the permission of the Preaching Resources division of Christianity Today International (www.PreachingToday.com and www.ChristianityToday.com).

RAISING CHILDREN ON PURPOSE:
Helping Your Children Find Their God-Given Calling
Updated and Expanded Edition

ISBN-13: 978-0-88368-997-4
ISBN-10: 0-88368-997-9
Printed in the United States of America
© 2001, 2006 by Wesley H. Fleming

1030 Hunt Valley Circle
New Kensington, PA
www.whitakerhouse.com

Library of Congress Cataloging-in-Publication Data
Fleming, Wesley H., 1955–
Raising children on purpose : helping your children find their God-given calling /
by Wesley H. Fleming.—Updated and expanded ed.
p.   cm.
Summary: "Enables parents to assess their children's God-given gifts and talents, recognize and encourage their spiritual passion, determine the point at which giftings and interests overlap, and help their children to discover and fulfill their callings in life"—Provided by publisher.
ISBN-13: 978-0-88368-997-4 (trade pbk. : alk. paper)
ISBN-10: 0-88368-997-9 (trade pbk. : alk. paper)
1. Child rearing—Religious aspects—Christianity. 2. Parenting—Religious aspects—Christianity.
3. Christian education of children. I. Title.
BV4529.F565 2006
248.8'45—dc22   2006001959

1 2 3 4 5 6 7 8 9 10 11 12   15 14 13 12 11 10 09 08 07 06

Contents

Appendices

Finding My Future in the Past

I grew up in the hills of upstate New York, on a farm my father leased to farmers in the area. I remember wishing I lived closer to my friends at school so I could play sports and have a more exciting social life. My path led me to a more contemplative life filled with daydreams and creative play. I planted fields with toy tractors, built cities with miniature trucks and cars, and launched models of rockets and futuristic spacecraft. My favorite imaginary play activity, however, was suiting up in my father's World War II army gear. Tripping over the cuffs of his U.S.-issue combat fatigues, with my head clanging inside a Japanese helmet, I'd disappear into full-grown cornfields to take on well-defended enemy strongholds, emerging from my mission only for lunch and dinner.

Years later, I would want to join the marines as a corpsman. I even visited navy recruiters the summer before my senior year of college. But God had other plans. In my last semester, I discovered that God had His own purpose for my life.

It's uncanny how my future can be observed in the past. As a church-plant pastor, I farm spiritual fields, build spiritual communities, launch leaders into the culture, lead God's army to take enemy strongholds, and tend to wounded warriors. The childhood expressions of my spiritual passion and gifting serve as guideposts to my unique path.

Before starting our church, I served as a minister of education (youth and children's pastor) for twenty-two years within local churches. In this role, it was my privilege to bind up brokenhearted families—parents and children who were wounded in life's battles. It was an honor to come alongside and guide teachers and parents who sought to plant seeds of destiny in their children so that each child might fulfill God's unique purpose.

As a parent, it has been a joy to help my children identify the origins of their unique paths and to prepare them for their callings. This book, and its related workshop ministry, Coming Home Ministries, find their beginnings in my quest to raise my children on purpose—according to their God-given purpose.

—Wesley H. Fleming

Beyond Food and Shelter

Along with food, shelter, love, and protection, a child has a basic need for a sense of purpose in life. Directionless kids tend to drift in the wrong direction. For hard proof, we have only to visit the local mall on a Friday night and observe the restless herd of young people aimlessly milling about experimenting with cigarettes and other "cool" behaviors. Kids who know that their lives have purpose and meaning strike a vivid contrast: They are enthusiastic, goal oriented, and responsible. One highly motivated teen put it this way: "Why get messed up in drugs and alcohol? I want to do something with my life."

The Bible says that before our children were born, God put within each of them a special plan for their lives—"a way they should go." The purpose our children are looking for lies within them! The Bible also says that we, as parents, have the distinct privilege of helping them find this calling and live it out. (See Proverbs 22:6.)

This book is dedicated to helping you, as a parent, raise up your children according to their God-given purposes. We offer practical support in two areas. First, we will help you to find your child's unique way; and second, we will assist you in cultivating your child's passion for living out that way.

Part I will show how you can discover your child's calling. An easy-to-use survey tool, called The DNA (Divine Notion Awaiting) Analysis, will assess your child's gifting and spiritual passion and then determine where they overlap. Our premise is that your child's calling is located at the place where his God-given gifting and spiritual passion intersect.

Part II will show you how to encourage your child to stay on his unique way. What good is it if your child knows the way he should go, but doesn't want to go there? To arouse in your child a passion for God and His will, you must do two things. First, you must help him develop a healthy capacity to trust, and second, you must help him form a positive impression of God the Father.

A healthy capacity to trust is essential for a vibrant and growing faith in God. Reaching out to God in faith requires an ability to trust and depend on another to meet one's needs. This faculty can be damaged if the bond of trust between parent and child is broken in childhood. Those, for instance, who were continually disappointed in the way their parents responded to their needs will be reluctant to give themselves away to God (the ultimate parent) and His plan for their lives, for fear of further disappointment.

In addition, your children need a positive impression of God, if they are to desire Him and delight in His will. They need to know Him for who He is—a loving, strong, dependable Father. They need an accurate concept of God in order to abandon all and follow Him.

For better or for worse, our parenting model provides our children with their first impression of God. When children are young, what we say is true, what we do is good, how we respond to their needs is love, and what we require is law. Children are poor discerners but excellent recorders—our example not only provides a first impression of God, but also a lasting one.

How do we develop in our children a healthy capacity to trust? How do we accurately represent the Father's love? We must meet their emotional needs.

For our children to trust in God's love and protection, they have to have experienced our love and protection. Our children reach out to us in faith to satisfy the longing of their souls. As we respond by faithfully meeting their needs, we strengthen their capacity to trust—and have faith—and also provide them with a model of God's character.

Meeting the emotional needs of your child lays a foundation for destiny. The task of the second half of this book is to identify the seven emotional needs of a child and to show you how to meet them.

God's perfect plan is for you to lead your children into their unique destinies. By discovering your children's callings and meeting their emotional needs in ways that reflect the Father's love and strengthen their capacity to trust, you can raise your children to fulfill their God-given purposes. Discover the "Jeremiahs," "Samuels," "Davids," and "Esthers" in your home, and encourage them to walk in their way!

PART I

Helping Your Child to Find His Way

Dear God,
When I grow up I want to be just like my Dad,
only not so hairy all over.
—Sam (age 6)

CHAPTER 1

God's Purpose for Parenting

WITHOUT A VISION

As I write these words, I am being summoned to an overflowing toilet in the upstairs bathroom. One of our children used too much toilet paper (again). "Where is the plunger?" I scream as water pours over the edge of the commode. "In the downstairs bathroom," my wife yells. I consider how easy it would be to write a book about parenting if I didn't have children.

Let me commiserate with my parent friends for a moment. (By "commiserate," I mean whine...)

Mom, wouldn't it be great if you could finally complete that college degree or just finish that cup of coffee you started? Aren't there times when you feel like your life is on hold, that your talents lie dormant, and that you have more to offer than cleaning up spills and changing diapers at two in the morning?

Dad, of course you'd do anything for your kids. Of course they mean the world to you, but now and then, between you and me, doesn't it seem like no matter how much you give it's never enough? Don't the constant demands of parenthood slow down your career progress, not to mention the love life you once shared with your wife?

Am I the only one who wonders what this parenting thing is about when dry cereal crunches beneath my bare feet as I make my way to the coffee pot in the morning? Am I the only one who needs to know that there is more to parenting than removing peanut butter from my preschool daughter's hair and chauffeuring my teens around town every Saturday afternoon? No, I think not. I believe that many of us need to know that what we are doing is not in vain—that there is great purpose for doing what we do on a daily, and nightly, basis.

Chances are you already have a purpose for parenting. You may not have articulated it, but you probably have one. What would you say it is? Circle the response that most closely reflects your own.

Your purpose for parenting:

a) I just want my kids to be happy and healthy.
b) I just want my kids to be happy and healthy, go to an Ivy League school, and make a six-digit income.
c) I just want to be happy and healthy and left alone for five uninterrupted minutes.
d) I just want to survive the next twenty years without hurting anyone.

Certainly Christian parenting is more than this—but what? Until we answer the question, we will parent more by accident than on purpose. In the absence of long-term goals, our daily parental concerns (in order of urgency) will be:

First: Are you bleeding?
Second: Where is your brother?
Third: What happened to the cat?

Is this the extent of your vision? Is crisis management the reason you sacrifice sleep and sanity?

The Bible says in Proverbs 29:18 that without a vision, the people will perish. Without a vision for parenting, our children's potential is likely to perish. Clean bedrooms and clean bottoms are noble aspirations, but if they constitute the full measure of our vision, we will surely limit our children's future.

So if there is a higher purpose for parenting, what is it?

GOD'S PURPOSE FOR PARENTING

Lucy asks that great philosopher of the comic strips, Charlie Brown, what her purpose is in life. He answers without hesitation: "Be kind. Don't smoke. Be prompt. Smile a lot. Eat sensibly. Avoid cavities, and mark your ballot carefully. Avoid too much sun. Send overseas packages early. Love all creatures above and below. Insure your belongings, and try to keep the ball low..." Before he can get out another platitude, Lucy interrupts: "Hold real still," she says, "because I am going to hit you with a very sharp blow upon the nose!"

To get beyond the platitudes and to the truth about parenting we need to consult the one who wrote "the Book." God, after all, is the ultimate parenting expert. He's been raising kids, ages one to one hundred one, for thousands of years. Among all the books on the subject, it's my opinion that the Bible is the definitive text on how to raise children. Even the language in which it was written offers insight.

The word for parent in Hebrew is *horeh*. The word for teacher is *moreh* and the word for God's teaching or instruction is *Torah*. These three words are derived from the verb *yarah*, which means "to throw, to cast, to shoot as an arrow." Our task, as parents, is revealed in the etymology of these words:

Parents (*horeh*) are teachers (*moreh*) who train their children in the Word of God (*Torah*) to fly like arrows (*yarah*) to a strategic and predetermined target.

The purpose of parenting is to train our kids in the Word and then send them to fulfill a specific kingdom purpose. Wow! Now that's a cause worth losing sleep over.

Psalm 127:4 supports the idea that parents are to send out their children like arrows. *"Like arrows in the hands of a warrior are sons born in one's youth"* (Psalm 127:4). The implication is this: *Parents are like warriors, in that they send their children (yarah), like arrows, to strike a strategic and predetermined target.*

What about the familiar verse, Proverbs 22:6? *"Train a child in the way he should go, and when he is old he will not turn from it."* Some mistakenly believe this verse teaches that if we inculcate our children with Christian beliefs, they are unlikely to go astray. If they should fall away, a parent need not be concerned, for it is only temporary. At some point, their moral training will reemerge and persuade them to return to their Christian heritage.

> The purpose of parenting is to train children to fulfill specific callings in the kingdom of God.

Though that is a popular interpretation of this verse, it's wrong. Many Scriptures advocate teaching our children the Bible, taking them to Sunday school, and memorizing the Ten Commandments (Deuteronomy 6:6–7, for instance), but this is not one of them.

Hebrew scholars agree that an accurate translation of Proverbs 22:6 is literally, "Train [start] a child according to his [the child's] way." This understanding implies that a child has a unique, God-given purpose in life. It suggests that each child has his own particular bent, talent, and disposition—in effect, his own calling or "way he is to go." Isaiah referred to this ordained way or course of life when he said, *"And thine ears shall hear a word behind thee, saying, This is the way, walk ye in it"* (Isaiah 30:21 KJV).

Respected Bible translator and commentator Derek Kidner supported this rendering when he stated that the verse implies "respect for [the child's] individuality and vocation." Kidner also observed that the word for "train" is elsewhere translated "dedicate" and may have that meaning here.[1] In this case, the verse suggests that parents are to set their children apart for God's calling.

Proverbs 22:6 instructs us to raise our children to enter their God-given callings—not whatever we may have chosen for them. Once our children have found their unique ways and are equipped to walk in them, the verse suggests that wild horses can't drag them away from them. A paraphrase of Proverbs 22:6 might read,

> Set your child apart for his God-given destiny, and when he matures and enters the path God has ordained for him, he will not want to leave it.

A Unique Calling

The Bible indicates that every child has a distinct calling upon his life—a predetermined target. God encourages Jeremiah, for instance, that before he was born, he was called to a special purpose. *"Before I formed you in the womb I knew you, before you were born I set you apart; I appointed you as a prophet to the nations"* (Jeremiah 1:5).

Paul states in Ephesians 2:10 that our children were born for a purpose—a predetermined work. *"For we are God's workmanship, created in Christ Jesus to do good works, which God prepared in advance for us to do."*

Perhaps, like many, you believed that only clergy could be "called." This may come as a shock, but the term *clergy* does not even appear in the Bible! It wasn't until the dark ages that the term was used to describe those who held office in the church. In all likelihood, those who sought to make a self-serving distinction between church leadership and the laity made its current meaning popular. (Incidentally, the term *laity*, which means "those of uniformed opinion," is not found in Scripture either.)

Though you may not be clergy, you are, according to Scripture, *"called"*—called to Christ (Romans 1:6), called out from those whose sole ambition is personal success and comfort (1 Corinthians 1:1–2), and called to an ordained and eternally significant purpose (Romans 8:28). In terms of parenting, we are called to help our children recognize their unique purposes and to send them to them. (See Psalm 127:4.) We are to help our children make their mark!

eↄeↄeↄ

From the age of three, Karen had wanted to be a nurse. When she gave her life to God as a teen and the desire persisted, she concluded it must be a calling. Her family, however, vigorously opposed her interest in the medical field. Her Mom and Dad were dedicated teachers. They insisted that education was the only way to change the world. Not only did they refuse to support Karen financially, but they also tried to discourage her by withdrawing from her emotionally.

After years of confusion, Karen finally decided that she would endure her parents' scorn and enroll in nursing school. She loved every minute of her studies and thrived in the hospital environment. Ironically, she did so well in her training that she not only got a full-time job as a nurse, but she was also asked to teach nursing part-time.

During a *Raising Children on Purpose* seminar, Karen was grateful to learn that the Bible taught that no man is to plan out the course of his or anyone else's life. According to the Bible, parents are to train a child according to the way God has created him to go. They are not to impose their desires upon their children, but to discover His will for them. A parent's wishes are not always God's will. The Bible says children should honor their parents, not blindly obey them. Karen honored her parents by considering their advice carefully, but they were not to determine her destiny. God alone put in her the "way she was to go."

We must be careful not to live vicariously through our children. Many armchair quarterbacks mandate an NFL draft upon their sons. Many middle-aged moms burden their daughters with unrealistic standards of fashion and beauty. Unreasonable parental expectations can devastate a child who dearly wants to please her parents and simply be loved for who she is.

A parent's role is not to mold but to unfold a child's potential. God gave our children unique purposes. Who are we to suggest different ones? Our goal as parents is to help our children to discover their God-given purposes and to train them to live them out, not to conform them to our plans for their future.

Good parenting recognizes a child's unique calling and sets him apart to fulfill it. It honors the child by customizing training to meet the child's specific needs and equipping him to fulfill his particular purpose.

> *A parent's role is not to mold but to unfold a child's potential.*

God has a special plan for you as well. As David said, *"All the days ordained for me were written in your book before one of them came to be"* (Psalm 139:16).

On the day you were conceived, God in heaven sat down to write a beautifully illustrated story. He drew pictures of a child growing up into adulthood and wove a gripping story line beneath each illustration. The angels were amazed at the detail and beauty of the pictures. They gasped in suspense as the plot unfolded. Unable to contain themselves, they stood to their feet and cheered as the child defeated his foes and arose victorious over his enemies. As the book came to its finish, all of heaven rejoiced over the happy ending.

Your life is a story, and God is the author. No two stories are the same—each has a special message to share. And every story was written on purpose—there were no mistakes or accidents.

Our children's lives are ordained. Our job is to help them get onto the right page so that their story unfolds into a beautiful adventure.

ARROWS OF DESTINY

Moses was like an arrow in the hand of a warrior. His parents sensed he was born for a divine purpose and did everything in their power to help him enter into it. They fearlessly opposed the most powerful man on earth and devised a plan to release their son's destiny.

By faith Moses' parents hid him for three months after he was born, because they saw he was no ordinary child, and they were not afraid of the king's edict. (Hebrews 11:23)

Like warriors, Moses' parents aimed their arrow straight at the enemy. Their careful aim helped to set their nation free from its oppressor and fulfilled God's purposes for their generation.

Israelite warriors in Bible times were committed to advancing God's purposes. Their arrows carried God's purposes forth toward a vital end. Our children are called to carry out God's purposes today. God has put in them a calling to advance the kingdom of God in their generation.

Psalm 127:5 confirms this. It says, referring to parents, *"They will not be put to shame when they contend with their enemies in the gate."* In Bible times, a city's gates were places of public business and litigation. Here a righteous man and his sons would fight for justice, truth, peace, morality, and generosity. Today, the gates of our cities are overwhelmed with corruption, lust, and fear. By raising children who fulfill their callings, these enemies of God will not prevail.

ᐸᐳᐸᐳ

John's parents saw in their son a gift to teach the Bible from a young age. "Even as a preschooler, he had to know everything," his mother recalls. "He'd never settle for a simple answer like, 'Well, that's just the way it is.' He had to know the reason for everything."

Besides an insatiable curiosity, another clue existed. At eighteen months, he was speaking in complete sentences. John not only needed to know the answer, but he needed to tell others. His mother recalls, "John has always been very vocal."

As John grew up, he was deeply drawn to spiritual things. His questions about God and the Bible were frequent and earnest, according to his parents. His parents fed his curiosity and gave him a steady diet of the best Christian authors and teachers they knew.

John's father prayed for his children every day to ensure God's plan for their lives. During his daily prayer walk, he'd routinely stop to kneel at a log along an old set of railroad tracks. There he would pour out his heart to God for his children.

How quickly the cause of Christ would triumph if every Christian home raised children who assumed their God-given callings.

Today, believers, church leaders, and even members of city government esteem John as an unusually gifted leader and powerful teacher. Currently, his church is building a library with Disneyesque features for the poorest inner city school in the district. Pillars with hieroglyphs and Egyptian-style statues will flank the entranceway. Inside, pupils will do research on the Internet in a lab that looks like a space shuttle. Students will study at tables in a "Renaissance cathedral," where light streams in from stained-glass windows. For group discussion, pupils will take a seat in a "Roman amphitheater." Books can be found in a prehistoric jungle complete with volcano, foliage, and dinosaur.

Last year, the church installed one thousand fire detectors in the homes of needy families, and periodically church members return to change the batteries. Twice each month food is taken to families in need all over the city. John is restoring the city gates. His success is due, in large part, to his parents' willingness to identify his calling and encourage him to pursue it.

Like warriors, John's parents sent their son, like an arrow, into the spiritual center of their hometown. Far from ashamed, they proudly watch him establish kingdom purposes for his city.

How quickly the cause of Christ would triumph if every Christian home raised children who assumed their God-given calling. Such a feat would release a flurry of divine purposes into the world, which would ignite a generation for Christ. Children raised to fulfill their calling as ministers of the New Covenant would bring God's kingdom to the church—revival would break loose! Children raised to fulfill their calling as businessmen would practice capitalism with a conscience. Children raised to fulfill their calling as scholars would challenge their colleagues with a logically consistent Christian worldview. Children raised to fulfill their calling to leadership would offer wise and moral guidance to our communities and nation. Our churches, our places of business, our educational system, and our nation would be restored! Raising children to fulfill their callings is a work of redemption:

> *They will rebuild the ancient ruins and restore the places long devastated; they will renew the ruined cities that have been devastated for generations.* (Isaiah 61:4)

The glorious purpose of parenting, according to the Word of God, is to raise children on purpose—their purpose. We are to help our children identify their callings and train them accordingly. This is God's vision for parenting. May it be our own.

Chapter Notes

1. Derek Kidner, *Proverbs*, Tyndale Old Testament Commentaries (Downers Grove, Ill.: InterVarsity Press, 1964), 147.

CHAPTER 2

DNA Shows the Way

In another *Peanuts* comic, Lucy contemplates the meaning of life with Charlie Brown. Lucy says, "Life is like a deck chair. Some place it so they can see where they are going; some place it so they can see where they have been; and some place it so they can see where they are at present." Charlie Brown's reply: "I can't even get mine unfolded."

Unfolding a life is no easy task. It's especially difficult if you are responsible for unfolding someone else's. Yet this is a parent's calling. Scripture tells us that we are to *"train a child in the way he should go"* (Proverbs 22:6).

Our dilemma is this: How do we raise a child to fulfill his calling when we have no idea what it is? Fortunately, God places in each of our kids a spiritual blueprint that, when properly interpreted, makes clear the way they are to go. To help you decipher this sacred data, this chapter introduces a unique tool—the DNA (Divine Notion Awaiting) Analysis Survey.

DNA: God's Blueprint for Destiny

Deep within the cell structure of our children is genetic information that determines everything from the size of their noses to their resistance to cancer. These microscopic strands of genetic data are called DNA. Every single hereditary characteristic of our sons and daughters is determined by this material. It was written into their chromosomes before they were born. DNA is a physiological blueprint for life.

There is another form of DNA that is less well known. You cannot see it with an electron microscope, and it is impossible for human beings to engineer. It is also formed in the womb and has an even greater determining force than biological DNA. It's spiritual DNA—our Divine Notion Awaiting—God's spiritual blueprint for life.

Like its biological counterpart, spiritual DNA possesses information about our children's unique potential. By carefully (and prayerfully) analyzing this prophetic code, we can collect and interpret data that reveals mysteries about our children's future.

The psalmist, David, recognized the existence of his spiritual DNA:

> *My frame was not hidden from you when I was made in the secret place. When I was woven together in the depths of the earth, your eyes saw my unformed body. All the days ordained for me were written in your book before one of them came to be.*
> (Psalm 139:15–16)

God's plan for David's life was recorded in his spiritual DNA. He would be a great leader of his people—a gifted king, a tremendous worship leader, and a powerful warrior. (See 1 Samuel 13:14.)

When Samuel called upon Jesse's family to anoint the next king of Israel, David was such an unlikely candidate that he was left to tend sheep in the field. Samuel, however, was a trained spiritual geneticist. He analyzed the DNA of David's brothers and found them lacking the characteristics he was looking for. With David, however, the tests came back positive!

Then the Lord said, "Rise and anoint him; he is the one." So Samuel took the horn of oil and anointed him in the presence of his brothers, and from that day on the Spirit of the Lord came upon David in power. (1 Samuel 16:12–13)

Thank God for Samuel's role in David's life. Without his guidance and skill, David might have continued to shepherd sheep instead of God's people.

How tragic it would have been if David had missed God's plans for his life. What if David's mother and father had imposed, with good intentions, a plan they thought was best for their son? Using subtle or perhaps overt means of manipulation, his mother and father could have undermined their son's God-given destiny.

God wants you to see the future in your children.

"No son of mine is gonna be some wimpy musician."

"What your father means, dearest, is there's no financial security in writing psalms. We'd hoped you would go to medical school like your brother."

What influence a parent wields! Like Samuel, you are called to be a prophet. God wants you to see the future in your children so that you can raise them to fulfill it. Often this involves confirming what a child knows to be true.

When God gave Jeremiah the results of his DNA analysis, he hoped the tests had been switched in the lab. He couldn't believe the Lord would call him to be a prophet. *"'Ah, Sovereign Lord,' I said, 'I do not know how to speak; I am only a child'"* (Jeremiah 1:6). It seems Jeremiah was a little apprehensive about God's plan for his life. He would have preferred to be a good ol' boy and simply fulfill the socially acceptable duties of a priest; but the Lord had something special in mind. Jeremiah had the DNA to be a prophet to the nations.

The Lord encouraged the reluctant young prophet not to be afraid of his unique call to preach hard truth to an unrepentant Judah. He confirmed Jeremiah's DNA test results: *"Before I formed you in the womb I knew you, before you were born I set you apart; I appointed you as a prophet to the nations"* (Jeremiah 1:5).

Like Jeremiah, our children have a specific call on their lives to fulfill a kingdom purpose. It was placed in them before they were born. And like Jeremiah, our children need to have their callings confirmed before they can confidently live them out.

So how do we analyze our children's spiritual DNA? You may recall that biological DNA is double stranded. Spiritual DNA, likewise, has two strands: spiritual passion and God-given gifts. Let's look at each component separately.

SPIRITUAL PASSION

Within a child there exist, in embryonic form, deep-rooted, innate desires that are God-given. They form the core motivation of his calling. We call these unique desires spiritual passion.

Let's look at some examples.

- Don used to read the encyclopedia for fun when he was ten. He had an insatiable appetite to learn how things worked. He also loved to hike and explore new trails and would spend hours out in the woods. Today, he chases down atomic particles for a living in a radiology lab. Don is a nuclear physicist.

- As a boy, John loved to gather up a group of kids in the neighborhood to play softball. He would encourage everyone on the team to new levels of performance with his enthusiastic cheers and screams. Today, he is a pastor.

- The majority of Nick's first five years of life were spent in a hospital. Born with a congenital heart defect, Nick's chest looked like a checkerboard from all of his surgeries. During his long stays, he would greet and encourage other children who were unfamiliar with the hospital environment. Today, he is a nurse.

- Katlin was always the champion of the underdog. The fact that she was petite made no difference if a boy was being bullied on the playground. Her peers considered her to be confrontational and at times aggressive. She also had the unsettling habit of always having to be right about everything. Today, she is a lawyer!

Because spiritual passion is undeveloped in childhood, it is a bit tricky to identify with certainty. My two-year-old nephew Aaron, for example, wants to be a truck when he grows up. I'm sure you'll agree that this is rather unlikely.

Spiritual passion is the fire that burns within us for our calling.

As children mature, their God-given interests come more clearly into focus and, if properly nurtured, eventually develop into their life's calling. A childhood interest in computers, for instance, may evolve into a passion for software engineering. A love for playing baseball may emerge into a passion for corporate loyalty or winning the most sales. An interest in playing with dolls and caring for younger siblings may grow into a passion for motherhood.

Spiritual passion remains consistent throughout life and should not be expected to change—though its expression may assume many different forms throughout a person's life. Research supports this. In a study by Rutgers University, eight-year-old boys were interviewed by educational specialists, and 20 percent of them (one out of five) accurately predicated the professions they would enter as adults.

Spiritual passion generates enthusiasm, dedication, and joy in performing a specific task. It is what children like doing. Very often, it causes them to excel in a particular area of performance and is readily observed in acts of outstanding achievement. It also motivates them to make an impact in the lives of others and is reflected in the positive response of those around them.

The Bible depicts spiritual passion in the lives of many of its heroes. Nehemiah was a cupbearer to the Persian king, but this was only the stage from which his destiny would be released. For seventy years, the city of his ancestors (Jerusalem) had laid in ruins as a result of Babylonian conquest. Now, under Persian rule, the exiles were permitted to return and rebuild their temple and city. When the calling of God comes upon Nehemiah to lead the restoration, he cries out before the king, *"Why should my face not look sad when the city where my fathers are buried lies in ruins, and its gates have been destroyed by fire?"* (Nehemiah 2:3). Nehemiah's passion to build and to lead is clearly evident: *"Come, let us rebuild the wall of Jerusalem, and we will no longer be in disgrace"* (v. 17).

> *Identifying our children's spiritual passion is the first step in helping them to determine their God-given purposes.*

Another example of spiritual passion is seen in the life of Jeremiah. Once God talks him out of his inferiority complex, his spiritual passion ignites and his calling to preach God's word begins to burn: *"His word is in my heart like a fire, a fire shut up in my bones. I am weary of holding it in; indeed, I cannot"* (Jeremiah 20:9).

Many other Bible characters demonstrate spiritual passion as well. Ezra demonstrates a passion to teach. Mary, the sister of Lazarus, shows a passion to worship. Sarah expresses a passion to be a mother. Paul presses on to spread the Word to the Gentiles.

Spiritual passion is the fire that burns within us for our calling. Identifying it within our children is the first step in helping them to determine their God-given purpose. The survey in the next chapter will assist us in this process.

Gifting

The second step in analyzing our children's spiritual DNA is to help our children identify their God-given gifts. This is accomplished by identifying their formally and informally recognized achievements and by observing the way they positively affect the lives around them.

Gifting is comprised of unique, God-given talents. These innate abilities within our children's spiritual DNA are what they do well. They are readily displayed in their accomplishments. Again, they may be reflected in a formally recognized achievement—your child may, for example, win a statewide spelling bee—or in an inconspicuous way—he may keep her desk drawers neat and well organized. Gifting can be observed in any activity or event that demonstrates unique ability, no matter how small—a simple bicycle repair job in your garage, for instance, or cheering up a friend after a game was lost.

Another way to identify our children's gifts is to observe the way they impact those around them. The Bible says that a man's gifts make room for him. (See Proverbs 18:16 KJV.) God-given gifts positively affect the lives they touch. They are the special "knack" our children have for improving the quality of life around them.

God's plan is revealed at the point where passion and gifting overlap.

For example, Linda shared that when she was younger, "People just seemed to get fixed when we talked." Wisely, she pursued a career in counseling.

Our children's gifts help them to carry out their spiritual passion. Gifts enable our children "to do" what they "want." They make our children's passions a reality.

God's plans for our children's lives are revealed at the point at which these two components of their DNA, passion and gifting, overlap. It is here that the longing of their souls to make a difference in people's lives (passion) meets with the ability (gifting) to make it happen.

The story of Eric Liddell, 1924 Olympic gold medallist for Great Britain, illustrates how a man's destiny is found at the point where gifting and passion cross. The 1970s movie *Chariots of Fire* chronicles Eric Liddell's Christian devotion and struggle to remain true to his faith in the midst of Olympic competition. In one scene, his sister appeals to him to return to his calling to the mission field. She worries that he has forsaken God's purpose for his life. Eric defends his decision to compete in the games by suggesting that his athletic prowess and passion to run are part of his calling. He earnestly contends, "When I run, I feel His pleasure."

Eric ran in the 1924 Olympics because that was what he was created to do—it was a part of his calling. His God-given passion to compete and his gifting to run met together on the track field. No wonder Eric felt the Lord's pleasure when he ran; he was fulfilling his destiny!

BIBLICAL EVIDENCE OF SPIRITUAL DNA

God's calling upon the great men and women in the Bible can be seen at the point where their gifting and passion overlap. David's calling to be a national leader and warrior, for instance, is seen in the gifts and passion of his childhood.

As a shepherd boy, David exhibited spiritual DNA when he protected his sheep from lions and bears and guided them to green pastures. David's passion to defend helpless sheep and his gifting to lead them to safety ultimately found expression in ridding the land of *"uncircumcised"* predators (Philistines) and shepherding God's people as a king. Ezekiel identified David's DNA when he said, *"I will place over them one shepherd, my servant David, and he will tend them; he will tend them and be their shepherd"* (Ezekiel 34:23).

We also observe David's spiritual DNA as a psalmist when he was a child. David's reputation as a talented musician and songwriter was widespread when he was only a young teen. One of Saul's servants recommended David to play in the king's court: *"I have seen a son of Jesse of Bethlehem who knows how to play the harp"* (1 Samuel 16:18). Years later David entered fully into his calling as a psalmist, writing many of the psalms in the Bible.

Events from Moses' youth reveal his spiritual DNA as a deliverer of God's people. His passion to deliver his people from slavery is apparent in his murder of an Egyptian taskmaster. Though murder was not part of God's plan for Moses, evidence of Moses' DNA is seen exactly at this point. It is here that passion and gifting overlap. Moses passionately longed to see his people free from the cruelty of Pharaoh. His blood boiled as he watched one of his own whipped unmercifully. Suddenly, he snapped. His God-given ability to take initiative and lead expressed itself, albeit out of God's timing, as he single-handedly delivered his Hebrew brother. (See Exodus 2:12.)

> *Destiny is not a place or an event, but a path that God has chosen for us to follow.*

Many of the disciples fished for fish in their youth before they fished for men. Mark 1:16–17 states, *"As Jesus walked beside the Sea of Galilee, he saw Simon and his brother Andrew casting a net into the lake, for they were fishermen. 'Come, follow me,' Jesus said, 'and I will make you fishers of men.'"* As they surrendered to their Master's plan for their lives, Jesus led them into the full expression of their DNA.

Esther's DNA (spiritual and physical) destined her to win a very important beauty contest. The first-place winner would become the queen of the wealthiest and most powerful country in the Middle East. As queen of Persia, Esther became aware of a sinister plot to destroy her people. She was hesitant to reveal the evil scheme to the king, however.

During a time in history when assassination attempts were a daily event, Persian law made uninvited guest appearances before the king a capital offense. Esther's reluctance to come before the king with her urgent news was understandable. Mordecai, Esther's spiritual parent and counselor, persuaded her to risk her life for the sake of her calling: *"And who knows but that you have come to royal position for such a time as this?"* (Esther 4:14).

God gifted Esther with the genes to be a beauty queen so she could someday save her nation. Her beauty, however, only set the stage for her destiny. It was her passion for her people and for her God that motivated her to fulfill her purpose.

Preface to Survey

Our children don't have to go through years of worrisome and costly soul-searching to discover God's purpose for their lives. We can help our children find direction early in life by recognizing their DNA—their Divine Notion Awaiting. This prophetic code lies deep within their souls. Tragically, in many cases, it remains a mystery unless parents are willing to engage in careful and prayerful DNA analysis.

This particular survey is designed for children and youth, ages seven to eighteen. For younger children, adjust the vocabulary to suit their understanding and skip questions that do not apply. For best results, a parent, parental guardian, or mentor should administer the survey. It is advisable to offer the DNA Analysis to your children at various times throughout their childhoods in order to update your understanding of God's intention for their lives.

Disclaimer: The "Way" Is Not a "Destination"

We do not suggest that the following survey will pinpoint a successful career for your child twenty years from now. Scripture tells us to help our children find "the way" they should go. The way is not a specific destination; it is a path. Destiny is not a place or an event. It is a path that God has chosen for our children to follow.

Though the survey may not allow us to determine in which branch of neurosurgery a child will specialize, we can discover the general direction he is to go. With knowledge of the child's "way" in hand, we can customize his training and provide the resources he needs for success.

PRAYER IS VITAL

One final comment before we begin. The purpose of this survey is to bring clarity to what God is willing to share with us about our children's callings. This means we are wholly dependent upon God to reveal the way our children are to go. He alone knows the story line of our children's lives. Helping our children find God's plan, therefore, is more a matter of prayer than survey.

Ask God for His leading as you seek to know God's will for your child. He has the plan and He promises to be found.

"For I know the plans I have for you," declares the LORD, "plans to prosper you and not to harm you, plans to give you hope and a future. Then you will call upon me and come and pray to me, and I will listen to you. You will seek me and find me when you seek me with all your heart. I will be found by you," declares the LORD. (Jeremiah 29:11–14)

CHAPTER 3

DNA Analysis for Ages 7–18

I. Survey of Gifts and Spiritual Passion

I n this section you will list events and activities in which your child has excelled. These achievements do not have to be formally recognized to be noted. They may be as simple as "makes friends easily" or "collects baseball cards"—mention any event or activity that clearly reveals special talent or ability. These may be things your child does consistently well or a single event that stands out in your mind. List these accomplishments chronologically, according to three age categories—preschool, elementary, and teen.

Sample Survey of Well-Performed Activities:

Preschool Age Examples:

1. Event/Activity: Starred as Mary in a preschool Christmas pageant.

2. Event/Activity: Arranges her toys neatly on her shelves.

3. Event/Activity: Wrote out pretend shopping lists and schedules for the day.

4. Event/Activity: Made up pretend math tests to give to her dolls.

5. Event/Activity: Saved her Easter candy for weeks.

6. Event/Activity: Won coloring contest.

7. Event/Activity: Learned to play songs on piano by ear.

Elementary Age Examples:

1. Event/Activity: Advanced to highest level in her Bible club class.
2. Event/Activity: Collected all six prizes from fast-food restaurant toy series.
3. Event/Activity: Makes jewelry and sells to relatives and friends.
4. Event/Activity: Cares for her pet rabbit without being asked.
5. Event/Activity: Saved up for bicycle and purchased it on her own.
6. Event/Activity: Assisted preschool teacher in Sunday school on regular basis.
7. Event/Activity: Started and organized a kids newsletter at church.

Teenage Examples:

1. Event/Activity: Swam competitively and won several meets.
2. Event/Activity: Started her own pet care and grooming business.
3. Event/Activity: Mowed lawns to save money for buying a car.
4. Event/Activity: Scored in top 20 percent in math SATs.
5. Event/Activity: Used a personal planner to organize the week.
6. Event/Activity: Taught four- and five-year-olds Sunday school by herself.
7. Event/Activity: Voted into student council.

RECORD OF WELL-PERFORMED ACTIVITIES

Child's name _____

List well-performed events and activities (add more spaces if needed):

During Preschool Years:

1. Event/Activity: _____
2. Event/Activity: _____
3. Event/Activity: _____

During Elementary Years:

1. Event/Activity: _____

2. Event/Activity: _____

3. Event/Activity: _____

During Teen Years:

1. Event/Activity: _____

2. Event/Activity: _____

3. Event/Activity: _____

Review the list with your child and ask for any additional accomplishments he or she feels were done well. Tell your child, "God has given you special abilities so that you can do many special things for Him. I want to help you to discover those special abilities." Many children are reluctant to share their achievements. (Some are not!) If you and your child disagree about what was "done well," the rule is to include it anyway.

II. GIFT AND PASSION INTERVIEW

1. Read aloud the list of well-performed activities from each age category. Ask your child which activities/events he considered "*really* enjoyable" or "the *most* fun." Underline them.

2. Referring to each underlined event/activity, ask the Interview Questions that follow. Record your child's responses in the spaces provided below. Add more spaces if needed.

   Note: Your child will naturally want to please you. She will want to give you the answers she thinks you wish to hear. Therefore, be careful to listen without making comment— except to clarify. Try not to sway your child's feelings about her achievements.

Interview Questions:

1. "What did/do you like most about the activity/event? In other words, what made/makes it so much fun for you?" (Address each activity/event separately. Use the following form to record responses. Underline any verbs and verb phrases that describe an action.)

    Follow up answers with probing questions until you have a satisfactory response. For example: "What do you like to do when you make models?" and "What, specifically, do you like to do when you play baseball?"

2. "What made you first like the activity/event?"

3. "What are you able to do that makes you so good at it?"

4. "If you had all the ability, money, brain power, equipment, time, and transportation you needed to do an even better job and have even more fun in the activity/event you mentioned, what would you do? What would be the next step in advancing in this activity/event?"

Sample Interview Record Form:

Sample responses of an 11-year-old boy

1. What did/do you like most about the activity/event? In other words, what made/makes it so much fun for you?"

    Sample response: "The thing I like best about basketball is getting together with my friends to play."

2. "What made you first like the activity/event?"

    Sample response: "I like hanging out with my friends."

3. "What are you able to do that made/makes you so good at it?"

    Sample response: "My coach says I am a team player. He says I'm great at rallying the team. I like to cheer them on."

4. "If you had all the ability, money, brain power, equipment, time, and transportation you needed to do an even better job and have even more fun in the activity/event you mentioned, what would you do? What would be the next step in advancing in this activity/event?"

Sample response: "I'd join the Chicago Bulls basketball team."

INTERVIEW RECORD FORM

(Remember to underline any verbs and verb phrases that describe an action.)

Activity/Event #1

1. "What did/do you like most about the activity/event? In other words, what made/makes it so much fun for you?"

2. "What made you first like the activity/event?"

3. "What are you able to do that makes you so good at it?"

4. "If you had all the ability, money, brain power, equipment, time and transportation you needed to do an even better job and have even more fun in the activity/event you mentioned, what would you do? What would be the next step in advancing in this activity/event?"

Activity/Event #2

1. "What did/do you like most about the activity/event? In other words, what made/makes it so much fun for you?"

2. "What made you first like the activity/event?"

3. "What are you able to do that makes you so good at it?"

4. "If you had all the ability, money, brain power, equipment, time, and transportation you needed to do an even better job and have even more fun in the activity/event you mentioned, what would you do? What would be the next step in advancing in this activity/event?"

Activity/Event #3

1. "What did/do you like most about the activity/event? In other words, what made/makes it so much fun for you?"

2. "What made you first like the activity/event?"

3. "What are you able to do that makes you so good at it?"

4. "If you had all the ability, money, brain power, equipment, time, and transportation you needed to do an even better job and have even more fun in the activity/event you mentioned, what would you do? What would be the next step in advancing in this activity/event?"

OBSERVATION QUESTIONS

Ask your child the following questions and record the verbs and verb phrases used in their responses.

(Address each activity/event separately.)
Example: When my child is engaged in this activity/event, he/she is usually <u>talking</u>, <u>mingling</u>, and <u>visiting</u>.

Regarding Activity/Event #1

When my child is engaged in this activity/event, he/she is usually _____, _____, and _____.

Regarding Activity/Event #2

When my child is engaged in this activity/event, he/she is usually _____, _____, and _____.

Regarding Activity/Event #3

When my child is engaged in this activity/event, he/she is usually _____, _____, and _____.

ACTION WORD TALLY

1. In the Action Word List below, list all the action words (verbs and verb phrases) underlined in the responses to the Interview and recorded in the Observation Questions. These "actions" are what your child likes to do. Because they are taken from activities/events in which the child excelled, they also represent the child's natural gifting.

    Note: Some action words reflect more than one gift. As a result, it will be easier to assess your survey if you record each appearance of an action word separately, even if it is repeated.

2. Using the Spiritual Gift List, below, determine and record the gift that is associated with each action word. Bear in mind the context of the action word when making your selection.

Action Word	Gift	Action Word	Gift
_____	_____	_____	_____
_____	_____	_____	_____
_____	_____	_____	_____
_____	_____	_____	_____
_____	_____	_____	_____
_____	_____	_____	_____
_____	_____	_____	_____
_____	_____	_____	_____
_____	_____	_____	_____
_____	_____	_____	_____

No Exact Match?

What if you cannot find an exact match between the action words your child used and those in the Gift List? In this case, bear in mind the context and approximate. Example: an eight-year-old boy used the following action words to describe his interest in making model planes: "glue, fit together, fasten." These verbs match or approximate the action words associated with the gift of craftsmanship: "assemble, construct, form." In another example, a twelve-year-old girl used the following verbs to represent her interest in horses: "feed, pet, hold, hug, brush, kiss, walk." These verbs match or approximate the Action Words associated with the gift of mercy: "care, love" and pastoring "take care of and guide." A final example: a thirteen-year-old boy used the following action words to describe his fascination with baseball: "get on the team, improve, get better, hit farther than before, do the best ever, cheer others on, make friends, encourage others to do their best." These action words are similar to "cheer, coach, and improve" found in the gift of encouragement and "gather together, join, belong" observed in pastoring.

SPIRITUAL GIFT LIST

Action words associated with the gift of **Administration***:*

list, straighten up, solve, manage, control, direct, oversee, govern, rule, carry out, organize, figure out, order, arrange, line up, prepare, measure, schedule, plan, collect, file, sort, set up, save, be on time, be attentive, record, remember, maintain

Action Words associated with **Craftsmanship***:*

set up, construct, make, design, invent, write, build, devise, assemble, put together, mold, form, beautify, embellish, adorn, fix/repair, improve, paint, create

Action Word associated with **Discernment***:*

know truth, make clear, clarify, simplify, clear up, summarize, solve, determine, resolve, decide, perceive, understand, judge, referee, arbitrate, discriminate, notice, sift, discern, distinguish, make decisions, correct, listen, think

Action Words associated with **Encouragement***:*

befriend, encourage, enthuse, inspire, bring hope, make happy, fill with courage or confidence, support, stimulate, spur, cheer, coach, push, challenge, promote, comfort, assure, urge, provoke, compel, incite, excite, exhort, talk, converse, improve, grow, develop, advance, progress, push to new heights and limits, relate to others, motivate

Action Words associated with **Evangelism***:*

persuade, compel, convince, win over, rescue, save, free, sell, tell with intent to persuade, win, reach, overcome, succeed, prevail, tell others

Action words associated with **Giving***:*

share, give, care, offer, provide, collect, contribute, stock up, save, give away

Action words associated with **Helps***:*

help, assist, support, aid, ease, relieve, take care of it, come to the rescue of, get things people need, serve, join

Action words associated with **Hospitality***:*

welcome, invite, host, greet, take in, charm, care, make small talk, love, chat, mingle, visit

Action Words associated with **Intercession***:*

pray, rescue, save, advocate, uphold, support, defend, make peace between, reconcile, appeal

Action Words associated with **Leadership***:*

lead, win as a team, call to action, tell others what to do, overcome, urge, contact, direct, invite, guide, demand, command, order, influence, initiate, start, see beyond present, see big picture, visualize, dream, take charge, go first, take others to new heights and limits, expect more from others and self, compel, improve, change, make happen, persuade, convince, inspire, make progress, advance, improve, excel, expect and give the best, correct the direction of

Action Words associated with **Music***:*

perform, play and make music, entertain, applaud, cheer, clap, sing, keep the beat, whistle, drum

Action Words associated with **Mercy***:*

show compassion, express kindness, show mercy, help, relieve, care, support, alleviate, lessen, ease, comfort, empathize, sympathize, pity, aid, soothe, calm, love

Action Words associated with **Pastoring***:*

direct, steer, lead, guide, comfort, take care of, mentor, equip, train, show how, help get ready, advise, counsel, gather together, round up, get together, team up, meet with, to be with friends, to make friends, join, belong, care, love, protect, defend

Action Words associated with **Preaching/Prophesy:**

preach, implore, plead, persuade, convince, warn, admonish, urge, caution, correct the behavior of, talk, speak, discuss, tell others to follow the truth, declare, reveal truth, perform well under stress, compete, speak truth

Action Words associated with **Psalmistry:**

worship, sing, compose, create, write music, exhibit, expose, reveal, manifest, represent, display, feel strongly about God, express, to be spontaneous, passionate, expressive, impulsive

Action Words associated with **Teaching:**

teach, figure out, instruct, clarify, explain, demonstrate, help others understand, inform, make known, tell others with intent to inform, be curious, investigate, study, read, research, discover, explore, look up, analyze, solve, examine, correct the knowledge of, learn, discover, observe, uncover, show, present, prepare to present, perform by presenting, display, illustrate, talk about things just learned, wonder why, ask, question, search, inquire

DNA ANALYSIS RESULTS

Your child's calling is found at the point in which gifting and spiritual passion intersect. The DNA Analysis shows certain spiritual gifts to be well represented by action words your child has used to describe his passion. These words, you will recall, are taken from activities/events in which your child has excelled—areas of giftedness. Taken together, these action words and their associated gift reveal your child's calling.

Fill in the first blank with the gift that appeared most frequently on your Action Word Tally, and the following spaces with gifts that are next most frequent.

God has called _____ (name of child)

to touch the lives of others through _____;

he/she also demonstrates a calling to minister in: _____,

_____, _____, and _____.

Examples:

> God has called Rachael to touch the lives of others through <u>craftsmanship</u>; she also demonstrates a calling to minister in <u>encouragement</u> and <u>mercy</u>.

> God has called Mickey to touch the lives of others through <u>encouragement</u>; he also demonstrates a calling to minister in <u>administration</u>.

DESTINY JOURNALS

To gain more insight into your child's Divine Notion Awaiting, find and save physical evidence of your child's spiritual DNA. Keep a scrapbook—A Destiny Journal—and treasure special awards, pieces of artwork, pictures, photographs of projects, and letters that reveal aptitude and interest. Among my most treasured finds is a math test that Rebekah made up and gave to her dolls when she was seven. Of the two dolls who took the test, one scored a B+ and the other a C. The test had several arithmetic problems and word problems—each doll answered separately. Rebekah had to have known the right answer to each problem to be able to correct the test. Not only does the test show Rebekah's passion and gift for teaching, but also her aptitude in math.

Description of God-Given Gifts

Administration: ability to plan and implement the goals of an organization, ensuring its successful operation. Biblical examples: Jethro (Moses' father-in-law) helped Moses to organize a board of elders through which he could better lead God's people (Exodus 18:13–26). Further Scripture references: 1 Corinthians 12:28; Acts 6:1–7.

Craftsmanship: ability to build, construct, design, manufacture, decorate, and produce objects of usefulness and beauty. Biblical examples: People known for their craftsmanship were selected to construct and adorn the temple (Exodus 31:2–11; 35:30–35; 2 Kings 22:5–6).

Discernment: ability to see the truth in a situation, to read between the lines and identify shades of gray, to grasp the bottom line. Biblical examples: Solomon used discernment to settle a dispute between two women who claimed to be the mother of a newborn baby (1 Kings 3:11–12, 16-28). Further Scripture references: 2 Chronicles 2:12; Psalm 119:125; Matthew 13:15–17.

Encouragement: ability to speak words of truth that comfort, inspire, and energize others. Biblical example: Barnabas, a missionary of the New Covenant, was called the son of encouragement (Acts 4:36). His influence revolutionized Mark's life and ministry (Acts 15:37–40; Colossians 4:10). Further Scripture references: Acts 11:22–24; Romans 12:8.

Evangelism: ability to share the gospel with unbelievers in such a way that those who hear are unusually receptive. Biblical example: Philip was referred to as an evangelist. He led an Ethiopian eunuch to the Lord (Acts 21:8; 8:27–39). Further Scripture references: Ephesians 4:11; Acts 2:41.

Giving: ability to contribute, with enthusiasm and joy, personal wealth to organizations that will further advance the purposes of God. Biblical examples: The church of Philippi was full of people who had the gift of giving, and Paul commended them: *"Moreover...not one church shared with me in the matter of giving and receiving, except you only; for even when I was in Thessalonica, you sent me aid again and again when I was in need"* (Philippians 4:15–16). Further Scripture references: Mark 12:44; Romans 12:8.

Helps: ability to assist others to meet their goals by offering practical support. Biblical examples: Paul commended Phoebe for being a great help to many believers (Romans 16:1–2). Further Scripture references: Romans 12:71; 1 Corinthians 12:28.

Hospitality: ability to make people feel welcome and accepted by providing basic comforts—kind conversation, refreshment, shelter, warmth, clothing. Biblical examples: Abraham's gift of hospitality was noted as he entertained three strangers (Genesis 18:2–33). Further Scripture references: Romans 12:13; 1 Peter 4:9–10; Hebrews 13:1–2.

Intercession: ability to pray with great compassion and perseverance for the needs of others, often followed by dynamic results. Biblical examples: Moses' gift of intercession was observed on several occasions as he appealed to God for mercy on behalf of Israel and spared them from judgment. In one instance, he asked God to deliver them from a plague of poisonous snakes.

> *The people came to Moses and said, "We sinned when we spoke against the Lord and against you. Pray that the Lord will take the snakes away from us." So Moses prayed for the people. The Lord said to Moses, "Make a snake and put it up on a pole; anyone who is bitten can look at it and live."* (Numbers 21:7–8)

Further Scripture references: Exodus 32:11–14; Numbers 14:13–20; Job 16:21; Ezekiel 22:30; 2 Corinthians 1:11; 1 Timothy 2:1–4.

Leadership: ability to see where to go and to bring others along. Biblical example: Nehemiah showed a gift of leadership as he led the people of Israel in a monumental effort to rebuild the walls of Jerusalem.

Then I said to them, "You see the trouble we are in: Jerusalem lies in ruins, and its gates have been burned with fire. Come, let us rebuild the wall of Jerusalem, and we will no longer be in disgrace." (Nehemiah 2:17)

Further Scripture references: Romans 12:8; Hebrews 13:17.

Music: ability to play a musical instrument well. Biblical example: Musicians used their gifting to give praise to God in the dedication of Solomon's temple (2 Chronicles 5:12–14). Further Scripture references: 1 Chronicles 9:33; 15:19–22; 2 Chronicles 35:15; Psalm 68:25.

Mercy: ability to alleviate the pain of others compassionately. Biblical example: Many of Jesus' healing miracles were the result of His mercy. Those who were shunned because of their illnesses were special recipients of mercy, i.e., those who were blind, leprous, demonized, and sinful (Mark 10:46–52; Matthew 8:3; 9:27–30; 15:22–28). Further Scripture references: Romans 12:8; Matthew 5:7; Luke 10:25–37; 17:12–14.

Pastoring: ability to gather and care for the needs of a group of people. Biblical example: David's leadership of Judah was pastoral. He was a gentle guide, yet capable of defending them ferociously. David prefigured Christ, the Good Shepherd, of whom God said, *"I will place over them one shepherd, my servant David, and he will tend them; he will tend them and be their shepherd"* (Ezekiel 34:23). Further Scripture references: Psalm 23; Ephesians 4:11–12; 1 Peter 5:1–4; John 10:1–18.

Preaching/Prophecy: ability to reveal and proclaim truth persuasively through various means of communication—verbal and nonverbal (Romans 12:6). Truth can be shared through conversation, lecture, visual illustration, object lessons, or drama. Prophecy is communicating God's intentions. Sometimes prophecy foretells the future; sometimes it simply "forth-tells" what is currently on God's mind. The latter context is called preaching.

Psalmistry: ability to express oneself to the Lord through a variety of artistic mediums and evoke worship from those who participate in the experience. Art forms may include music, banners, dance, lyricism, and drama. Biblical example: David wrote many of the psalms and was consistently seen worshipping the Lord with all his might. As the ark was brought into the house of the Lord, David led the people of Israel in expressive, spontaneous, heartfelt worship.

> *David, wearing a linen ephod, danced before the LORD with all his might, while he and the entire house of Israel brought up the ark of the LORD with shouts and the sound of trumpets.*
>
> (2 Samuel 6:14–15)

Further Scripture references: Exodus 15:20; 1 Chronicles 16:7; Psalm 150; Ephesians 5:18–20.

Teaching: the ability to comprehend a complicated truth and clearly communicate it to others such that understanding occurs and behavior is changed. Biblical example: Apollos, a Jew from Alexandria, demonstrated a gift of teaching. The Bible refers to him as *"a learned man, with a thorough knowledge of the Scriptures"* (Acts 18:24) and says that he *"spoke with great fervor and taught about Jesus accurately, though he knew only the baptism of John"* (v. 25). What makes his gift of teaching most apparent was not his ability to teach, however. It was his ability to be teachable. Apollos loved to learn. *"When Priscilla and Aquila heard him, they invited him to their home and explained to him the way of God more adequately"* (v. 26). Further Scripture references: Mark 4:2; Mark 4:33; Ephesians 4:11; Romans 12:7; 1 Corinthians 12:28–29; 2 Timothy 2:2.

Please refer to Appendices A–D to help determine your child's special calling.

The Destiny Survey Chart in Appendix A shows the intersection of gifts and passion and how they combine to reveal a child's calling. It also provides additional questions that can assist your child in understanding his or her spiritual DNA by helping you to gather input and observations from other people who are close to your child. Fianally, the chart may be used as a handy reference in summarizing your child's gifts and spiritual passion.

Appendix B, "The Four-Temperament Model of Human Behavior," helps you identify your child's unique personality style.

Appendix C, "Discovering My Story," gives you a chart to combine your findings for an overview of your child's gifts, passion, and temperament.

Appendix D, "Identifying Vocation Based on Gifts, Passion, and Temperament," helps you to see the relationship between your child's gifts, passion, and personality and the potential vocations through which he may fulfill his calling.

CHAPTER 4

Four Benefits of Raising Children on Purpose

"FINDING MYSELF"

I remember returning from college one semester to tell my parents I had changed my major again. "He just needs to find himself," my mother said to my father sympathetically. My dad was not convinced. He was sure I had found my purpose in life: to spend all of his money!

I decided to major in "finding myself" and became a philosophy student. Although it was a four-year school, I took five years to complete my degree (I wanted to do a thorough job). After several costly career placement exams, I was still clueless. Finding my purpose in life was a time-consuming and expensive experience.

When I became a Christian my last semester during senior year (thank God for that extra year), one of the first things that got me excited was the idea that God had a purpose for my life. As God gradually revealed it to me, I became motivated, goal-minded, and, little by little, more responsible. My mother was so amazed she became a Christian herself!

So much precious time, energy, and resources could have been saved had I known the way I was designed to go. I'm committed to

helping my kids discover God's calling. I want to raise them on purpose—their purpose—so that they are motivated, responsible, peak
performers, and so that they won't spend all my money!

Helping our children to know their way provides four distinct
advantages: our kids will be motivated, they will perform well, and
they will enjoy job satisfaction and experience job security. Let's look at
each of these benefits separately.

#1 MOTIVATION

Harry Truman once said, "I've found the best way to give advice
to your children is to find out what they want and then advise them
to do it." Children who are raised
according to their callings are
encouraged by their parents to
pursue what they were made to do.
They are trained to do those things
they love to do and are naturally
talented to perform well. As a

*When training focuses on children's
abilities, then minimal coaching
and prodding are needed.*

result, they are eager and enthusiastic. Parents help their children to
make their avocations their vocations.

Everyone loves to do what he or she is good at! Kids enjoy success as much as adults. Success breeds more success. When training
focuses on our children's abilities, rather than their limitations—their
likes, rather than their dislikes—minimal coaching and prodding are
needed. Children who are raised on purpose are self-motivated.

Give my daughter Rachael an art project and she's wired for 220.
Give her a math problem and it's as if someone just pulled the plug.
Chronic fatigue syndrome sets in. No doubt, she will have to learn
math, but mixing into the curriculum a generous dose of creativity (her
passion) helps make the medicine go down.

Giving her the big picture helps as well. Throwing pots, framing pictures, painting landscapes, and mixing paints all require a generous understanding of math. Within the context of her calling, math takes on new meaning.

The secret of self-discipline is motivation. When our children are excited about fulfilling their calling, discipline takes care of itself.

A mason was astounded by how fast his partner was laying brick for a new hospital. "Hey Joe, what's the deal? It's just another building."

His friend replied, "Oh no, it's not. My wife is eight months pregnant and we're building the maternity ward."

When a goal has personal meaning, we are willing to muster the discipline needed to accomplish it. Children who are in touch with their callings are goal-minded. They are engaged in activities that they feel passionate about, and self-discipline comes naturally.

It took a Marine Corps reveille to get Joe (seventeen) out of bed most mornings. Yet he set his own alarm and rose at the crack of dawn when it was his day to intern at the local vet.

Rebekah (thirteen) told her guidance counselor that she wanted to take German. The counselor replied, "German is a hard language. I think you'd be better off with Spanish or French at your age." Rebekah persisted, "But my friend who works at the zoo told me that German was a better language for getting my Ph.D. in zoology." The guidance counselor got really quiet.

#2 PEAK PERFORMANCE

Two fathers were bragging about their sons.

"What's your boy going to do after college?" asked the first.

"He's going to be a lawyer," said the second dad. "He's naturally gifted for it."

"How's that?"

"Well," the father replied, "he is always putting his nose into other people's business, so he might as well get paid for it."

☙☙☙☙

We excel at what we are good at. Not so profound, but a powerful concept nonetheless. When our children are trained to perform in their areas of giftedness, success is almost inevitable. For example, the administratively gifted child trained in organizational systems is likely to become an excellent administrator. The leader trained in communication skills and motivational psychology is likely to be a successful leader. Children who are raised on purpose—according to their gifts and passion—naturally excel.

Conversely, when children are expected to perform in areas in which they are not gifted, success is usually marginal. A child's self-esteem may be threatened as well. Jake, for instance, was required to study conversational French for four years despite the fact that he had a speech impediment. He dreaded the class so much he developed panic attacks and dropped out of school

> *When children are trained to perform in areas of their giftedness, success is almost inevitable.*

for a time. Now, I'm not suggesting we always excuse our children from areas of training that are outside their gift zones. Basic math and language skills are needed to fulfill a calling in almost any field. My point is this: Focus on your child's gifting, and success will breed success. Train the child gifted in discernment in counseling skills and raise a top-notch Christian counselor. Train the child gifted in craftsmanship in structural design and raise a Spirit-filled architect.

When Caleb was in fifth grade his teacher said he was "weak" in language arts and that he should go to summer school for a writing skills course. Caleb was mortified. Summer school was for the kids who had real problems, he believed. Realizing Caleb's strengths were in mathematics and his passion was computers, his parents gave him a choice. He could take the writing skills course, or he could take a computer language course with the following condition: He must keep a diary of everything he learned that day, writing two pages each evening. His parents corrected the entries the next day and reviewed them. Caleb had no problem with the assignment. Not only did his writing improve, but his computer knowledge grew as well.

What is a "weakness" anyway? Isn't it simply the absence of strength? Just because you don't skate as well as Scott Hamilton doesn't mean you are a weak skater. If you aren't a software genius like Bill Gates, it doesn't mean you are necessarily computer illiterate. No! The absence of gifting does not imply weakness, nor should it bring shame. It suggests that your gifting lies somewhere else. A so-called weakness simply means, "Look elsewhere for my destiny!"

The absence of gifting in an area does not imply weakness, nor should it bring shame.

The following parable illustrates my concern about our tendency to focus on "weaknesses." Once upon a time, a group of animals met together to figure out how they could best prepare their children for the future. They opened a special school to teach their offspring to succeed in "the jungle out there." Each child would be trained in four survival skills: running, jumping, flying, and swimming.

The fish washed out in the first subject. Though he was a great swimmer, he was horrible at running. No matter how hard his teachers drilled him, he only flopped around during the class. The other kids made fun of him, and he was so humiliated that he vowed never to try to excel at anything again.

The rabbit fared better. He scored well in jumping and running, and he even passed swimming, but no matter how many trees he jumped out of, he couldn't seem to get the hang of flying. Even though he got good grades in the other subjects, his parents were extremely upset that he had failed flying. He felt he was a terrible disappointment to them and was angry and ashamed of himself.

The deer performed beautifully in running and jumping and almost seemed to fly, but swimming was her downfall. Her parents and teachers spent hours training her to swim. No one seemed to care how well she did in her other subjects. She eventually got discouraged and let her other grades fall.

God's focus is on turning your child's strengths into greater strengths.

The eagle had a strong personality and was a natural-born leader. When he tried to jump, however, he tripped over his wings and fell. All the animals laughed at him. He got mad and started to cause trouble. He gathered all the other eagles together and started a gang. The eagles would strut about the neighborhood and schoolyard pecking at classmates and making everyone miserable.

After the year was over, the teachers, administrators, and parents of the school got together. They concluded that the eagle had "at-risk behavior," that the fish was an underachiever, the deer was depressed, and the rabbit had a fear of heights. So they hired a school psychologist and continued the training course the following year.

Moral of the story? Focus on the strengths of your children and you raise up motivated and successful young men and women. Focus on their weaknesses and you raise up children who are demoralized, full of shame, and misdirected.

God gave our children strengths; He did not give them weaknesses. He is not concerned about turning weaknesses into strengths;

He is interested in turning strengths into greater strengths. The Bible tells us to build upon our children's gifts, training them up in "the way they are created to go."

God did not, for instance, try to make David a better book-keeper—census taking was definitely not his forte. He trained him in leadership—*"He trains my hands for battle; my arms can bend a bow of bronze"* (Psalm 18:34)—so he would become a great warrior and king.

God has made each of us good at something. The apostle Peter said, *"Each one should use whatever gift he has received to serve others"* (1 Peter 4:10). Your child awaits your help to develop this gift. By focusing training efforts upon areas of natural gifting and interest, instead of areas of "weakness," you assure your child a greater degree of excellence in his calling.

#3 Job Satisfaction

A mother was having a hard time getting her son to leave for school one morning. "Nobody likes me at school," said the son. "The teachers don't and the kids don't. The superintendent wants to transfer me, the bus drivers hate me, the school board wants me to drop out, and the custodians have it in for me. I don't want to go."

"You've got to go," insisted the mother. "You're healthy. You've got something to offer others. You're a leader. Besides, you're forty-nine years old, and you're the principal!"

So many believers feel trapped in dead-end, dreary jobs. So few have found their unique, passion-filled purpose in life. Research shows that as many as three to four out of every five men and women are in jobs that are not right for them.

When you consider that we spend more time at work than in any other activity during our waking hours, the amount of discontent in the work place is an American tragedy. Initiative and enthusiasm are virtually unknown in many employment settings. People live for the weekends. Others bide their time until retirement. So often we hear, "I hate my job, but it pays the bills."

A study of 4,126 male corporate executives, conducted by Jan Halper, Ph.D., showed interesting results. Fifty-eight percent of all middle managers said that despite years of striving to achieve their professional goals, their lives seemed "empty and meaningless." Sixty-eight percent of senior executives said that they had neglected their family lives to pursue professional goals, and half said they would spend less time working and more time with their wives and children if they could start over again.[1] These sentiments sound a little like Solomon, who once said,

> *Yet when I surveyed all that my hands had done and what I had toiled to achieve, everything was meaningless, a chasing after the wind; nothing was gained under the sun.*   (Ecclesiastes 2:11)

God's heart must break to watch sincere Christians waste their lives away. So many never tap into their God-given abilities and passions. His calling on their lives lies dormant and undiscovered.

Children who are raised according to their purposes are guaranteed that their vocations are not meaningless. They are nothing less than callings from God. God's career path employs their natural talents and deepest interests. He makes sure their avocations becomes their vocations. *"See to it that you complete the work you have received in the Lord"* (Colossians 4:17).

#4 ETERNAL JOB SECURITY

Was Jeremiah ever unemployed? Was Moses ever fired from his job? Was Esther ever useless and ineffective in her vocation? Despite horrible economic conditions, wicked bosses, and stubborn subordinates, the heroes of the Bible were always employed. God says His gifts and calling are irrevocable. (See Romans 11:29.) He does not fire or lay off those who follow His will. No matter how desperate the circumstances, Paul was always employed and forever striving for a final promotion:

> *Brothers, I do not consider myself yet to have taken hold of it. But one thing I do: Forgetting what is behind and straining toward what is ahead, I press on toward the goal to win the prize for which God has called me heavenward in Christ Jesus.*
>
> (Philippians 3:13–14)

Job security is at a premium today. Forty years ago, twenty-five years of service to a company was common. You'd get a gold watch and a fat pension. Today, if you are lucky enough to work five years for the same company, you may get a cheap HMO. Yet if God employs our children, they have eternal job security and free health and life insurance.

Raising our children according to their purposes insures them jobs with Heaven, Inc.—the most solvent corporation in the universe.

Raising our children according to their purposes insures them jobs with Heaven, Inc.—the most solvent corporation in the universe. They answer to J.C. (the greatest CEO of all time). He will see to it that they are never without rewarding work. He will precisely match their passions and giftings to their careers. That doesn't mean work will always be easy. He may give them some tough assignments. He may insist on some challenging on-the-job-training or temporarily reassign them to a less desirable position for resource development, but one thing will not change: Our children will always be employed. God has never fired or retired anyone, *"for God's gifts and his call are irrevocable"* (Romans 11:29).

A woman took her four-year-old with her to work one day. Though ordinarily shy, he seemed eager to meet each of her coworkers. After the introductions were over, however, he was clearly unhappy. Going home, the mother asked her son what was troubling him. "I never got to see the turkeys, clowns, and rats you said you worked with," he complained.

Many of us have become negative, cynical, and apathetic about our work. Yet our work is sacred to God. It's our calling, and for some, it still awaits discovery. God has a purposeful life for us to lead, and we are to live it out in our vocations.

> *For we are God's workmanship, created in Christ Jesus to do*
> *good works, which God prepared in advance for us to do.*
>
> (Ephesians 2:10)

Chapter Notes

1. Jan Halper, Ph.D., *Quiet Desperation: The Truth about Successful Men* (New York, N.Y.: Warner Books, 1988), 16.

PART II

Helping Your Child to Stay on His Way

The teacher asked her students what they wanted to become when they grew up. "President." "A fireman." "A teacher." One by one they answered until it was Billy's turn. The teacher asked, "Billy, what do you want to be when you grow up?" "Possible," Billy responded. "Possible?" asked the teacher. "Yes," Billy said. "My mom is always telling me I'm impossible. When I grow up, I want to become possible."

CHAPTER 5

Lighting a Fire by Warming a Heart

O ur desire for God determines our destiny. Saul, you will remember, fell short of his calling for one reason. Despite the fact that he had many of the attributes of a king of Israel, he lacked one essential quality: a heart for God. Saul's intelligence, gifting in leadership, and physical stature were of little concern to a sovereign God who can do a little with a lot, a lot with a little, and everything with nothing. *"But now your kingdom will not endure; the Lord has sought out a man after his own heart and appointed him leader of his people, because you have not kept the Lord's command"* (1 Samuel 13:14). A heart for God—this determines the success with which we meet our calling. God chose David to be king over His people because of the size of his heart, not the size of his body, bank account, or IQ. Those who are consumed with a desire to know Him and serve Him will fulfill their callings and establish His purposes on earth.

> *For the eyes of the LORD run to and fro throughout the whole earth, to show himself strong in the behalf of them whose heart is perfect toward him.* (2 Chronicles 16:9 KJV)

So it is with our children. The fulfillment of their callings depends upon their passion for God. When kids want God with all their hearts, nothing can stop them from accomplishing His plan for their lives.

Commit to the LORD whatever you do, and your plans will succeed. (Proverbs 16:3)

Kerry was in seventh grade when she shared with me how she wanted to be a foreign missionary. She was a frail and painfully shy girl, and were it not for her incredible desire to please God, I would have doubted what she believed was her calling. Today, we receive mail from her mission station in Ecuador where she teaches orphaned children about the love of God. While in our youth group, Kerry's life was transformed before our eyes. We watched her change from a timid little girl to a faith-filled woman of God. She led Bible studies, worship, and outreaches, risking comfort and security for more of God. God seemed to work in her life in proportion to her tenacious love—and she would tell you, He had quite a work to do. Kerry is fulfilling God's amazing plan for her life! Why? It's not because she has a strong constitution or a dynamic personality. Kerry is successful because she has been taken over by God's love.

The child who loves God will do His will.

The child who loves God will do His will. She will conform her character to His image because she desires to please Him. She will learn His Word and yield to His correction and training because she seeks to make Him proud. She will risk comfort, security, and convenience to follow Him because she trusts Him. Character growth, Bible knowledge, and vocational skill will develop naturally out of her love for Jesus.

When kids love God, they want the Holy Spirit to work in their lives and unfold their destinies. They want Him to be their guide, teacher, and source of provision. Cultivating a hunger for Jesus is the most effective thing we can do to assure our children's callings.

Information gathered from the DNA Analysis Survey has helped our children to know the way they are to go; yet this knowledge is of little value if they are not interested in going there. Discovering our children's God-given calling is only the first step in raising them on purpose.

What can we do to help our children fall in love with Jesus? Lighting a fire for God in our children begins by warming their hearts. By faithfully meeting our children's needs for love and security, we powerfully determine their interest in God and ability to relate to Him.

Warming Their Hearts by Meeting Their Emotional Needs

A healthy capacity to trust is the most important gift parents can give to their children. The ability to depend on another for one's needs is essential for conducting intimate relationships—both human and divine. Without trust, vulnerability and interdependency are impossible.

Children who grow up in warm, stable, loving environments where it is safe to be honest and exposed, and where emotional needs are met, develop an ability to trust. In homes like these, trust is rewarded and grows. It is here that children learn the reasonableness of giving themselves away to God and connecting with others on an emotional level.

In homes where there is a great deal of hurt and disappointment, children are less likely to consider trust a safe option. When these children grow up, they are predisposed to manage their lives in their own strength, apart from God's involvement.

In the following testimony, Kay Arthur, president and principal teacher of Precept Ministries, an internationally acclaimed Bible study ministry, credits her parents' love for her capacity to depend on God during the most difficult time in her life.

When Kay's first husband died, her life was shattered. She was suddenly a single parent with two sons to raise and a mortgage to pay off. After a long, hard day at work, she would return home overwhelmed by grief and fear of the future. In the midst of her despair, she recalls her father's love.

I loved my daddy's arms and welcomed any opportunity to be in them. When I skinned my knees—which happened frequently for this tomboy—I'd run to Daddy. Or in the evenings, sometime between doing the dishes and finishing my homework, I'd often curl up in his lap, lean my head on his chest, and feel so secure....

I wished I were a little girl again. I wished I had someone to hold me, to tell me that everything would be all right and reassure me that I'd survive.

As I turned to walk in the house, I suddenly saw in my mind's eye a little girl in pigtails flying down a vast marble corridor. Oil paintings bigger than life hung on the walls. As she dashed by, I could almost hear her little shoes clicking on the marble floor. Tears flooded her eyes and overflowed, leaving white streaks on her dirty face. Blood trickled down her skinned leg, making a path in the dirt and gravel embedded in her knee and shin. She called for her daddy and sobbed as she ran.

It was a long corridor. At the end two huge gold doors glistened in the sunlight that filtered through beveled cathedral windows. On either side of the imposing doors stood two magnificently dressed guards holding huge spears and blocking the entrance into the room beyond.

Undaunted, the little girl ran straight toward the doors, still crying, "Abba!" She never broke her stride, for as she neared the doors the guards flung them open and heralded her arrival: "The daughter of the King! The daughter of the King!"...

Oblivious to everything going on around her, she ran past the seven burning lamps of fire and up the steps leading to the throne, catapulting herself into the King's arms. She was home, wrapped in the arms of his everlasting love. He reached up and, with one finger, gently wiped away her tears. Then he smoothed the sticky hair on her face back into her braids, tenderly held her scuffed leg, and said, "Now, now, tell your Father all about it."

I walked into my house, went to my bedroom, and got on my knees.

Never once have I had a hard time telling my heavenly Father all about it. Never once have I feared he would push me away. My daddy never did and neither did my mother, so why would God?[1]

By faithfully meeting Kay's needs for love and safety as a child, her parents reinforced and strengthened her natural capacity to trust and laid a foundation for childlike dependence upon God. Kay was able to receive the love and strength of God because she had experienced it before.

When trust is broken, a child's ability to initiate and maintain intimate relationships, both human and divine, is compromised.

Rich's mother was short-tempered and easily irritated when he was growing up. As a child, he was frequently the target of her explosive anger. Her unpredictable mood made it difficult for Rich to fully rely on her for his emotional needs.

My mom seemed to be mad all the time. I knew she loved me, but I was always tense around her. I couldn't really trust her. Now, I'm an adult and I still have trouble trusting. I know in my head that God wants to take care of me, but I have trouble letting go. I feel like I have to meet my own needs to stay safe.

When a child's emotional needs go unmet, perhaps because a parent is preoccupied with his or her own needs—or is absent or abusive—the child's capacity to trust is damaged. Rich, for instance, was repeatedly disappointed as he reached out to depend on his mother for love and protection. He now believes on an emotional level that trusting in others to meet his needs is unsafe and too great a risk. His reluctance to trust spills over into his relationship with God, where the idea of giving up control to a parent figure is especially frightening.

> *Cultivating our children's faith in God starts with cultivating our children's faith in us.*

Unmet emotional needs hamstring destiny. A parent who is unable or unwilling to tend to a child's emotional needs conveys the message that depending on others is not safe. Unless this belief is changed, the child is likely to turn to manipulation and control as a means of relating to others and to God, rather than healthy interdependence.

꿈꿈

Shelly's marriage was in trouble. She was jealous of her husband's friendships and interests outside the home. She refused to share a joint bank account and insisted on filing her income tax separately, even though it would have been more advantageous to file together. Her husband complained that she was controlling, defensive, and quarrelsome. What was the root of Shelly's emotional difficulty?

Shelly's father left her mother for another woman when she was ten years old. The emotional pain she experienced in the wake of her father's abandonment, the ensuing demise of the family's finances, and the public humiliation of her mother severely damaged her capacity to trust others. Depending on God was particularly difficult for her because He represented a father figure. The prospect of opening up her heart and getting hurt again by another father was too much for her.

Though her heavenly Father longed to care for Shelly, she preferred to fend for herself emotionally. "I've always felt like I had to take care of myself," she shared. "It's hard to stop now and rely on my husband, let alone God."

Cultivating our children's faith in God starts with cultivating our children's faith in us. Our children look to us and ask, "Will you meet my needs? Can I trust you?" As we respond by meeting their needs, we say, in effect, "Yes, have faith in me. It's going to be okay. I'll take care of you." By rewarding their trust, we develop in our children a capacity to have faith—an ability to believe in another to care for their needs. Our children conclude, "I can depend on you to meet my needs. I can have faith in you and not be disappointed. I believe in you." As they begin their Christian lives, their capacity to trust is called upon by God, who requires faith in all aspects of His relationship with them. Hebrews 11:6 confirms, *"And without faith it is impossible to please God, because anyone who comes to him must believe that he exists and that he rewards those who earnestly seek him."*

For all intents and purposes, the parent-child relationship is a role-play of our relationship with God. God uses it to prepare us for a relationship with Him. As we affirm our children's trust in us, we teach them that faith in a parent figure is a reasonable way to manage their needs.

THE ORIGINS OF TRUST

Children are born with a natural ability to trust. They instinctively assume their parents are dependable and safe. Indeed, they have no choice but to depend on their mothers and fathers; it's a matter of survival.

Each of our children was breast-fed. Soon after they arrived in this world, they turned their little heads in a slow and quivering motion toward their mother's chest in search of nourishment and life. In faith, they reached out their tiny fists to grab hold of their life source. They were not disappointed. Over the years, we have tried to continue to reinforce their trust in us.

Our goal is to make sure our children always view trust as a reasonable means of managing their needs. Their ability to maintain an intimate relationship with God and others depends on it.

Our children's capacity to trust is not indestructible. Neglecting their need for understanding, focused attention, or respect can damage trust and impair their ability to depend on others in the future. It is crucial that we support our children emotionally if we want our children to know emotionally, as well as theologically, that putting their faith in Jesus is the smart thing to do.

> *Our goal is to make sure our children always view trust as a reasonable means of managing their needs.*

A child whose capacity to trust has been well reinforced by her parents is well prepared to trust in God. She has been raised to see the reasonableness of depending upon those who are faithful and who offer resources beyond her own. She has the freedom to trust and receive help, comfort, strength, and provision from God and others. Because it was safe to depend on her parents for her needs, she is able to look to God—the ultimate parent figure. Jill Briscoe, author and speaker, shares how her father's love helped her to find God's comfort as an adult.

Though I was barely six years of age, I well remember sitting by a roaring fire on a Sunday during World War II. Our family had fled the bombs that rained down on us one night, chasing us hundreds of miles away to the beautiful English lake district—William Wordsworth country.

The mists were gone, and a storm had broken over our heads. The rain, like giant tears, slashed against the windowpane, and the thunder grumbled away as if it were angry it had to hang around all day. I didn't like storms, and I was old enough to understand that a bigger storm was raging, a war involving the entire world. But at the moment, it seemed far away. The fire was warm, and my father was relaxed, reading the paper, sitting in his big chair.

Suddenly, as if he were aware I needed a bit of reassurance, he put down his paper and smiled at me. "Come here, little girl," he said in his quiet but commanding voice. And then I was safe in his arms, lying against his shoulder and feeling the beat of his heart. What a grand place to be. Here I could watch the rain and listen to the thunder all day.

I've realized how my heavenly Father shelters me from the storms of life. When times of sorrow swamped me at my mother's funeral, I sought the reassurance of my Father's presence. When winds of worry whipped away my confidence as I faced gangs of young people in street evangelism, I glanced up to see my Father's face. When floods of fear rose in my spirit as I waited in a hospital room for the results of frightening tests, I sensed my heavenly Father saying, "Come here, little girl."

I climbed into his arms, leaned against his shoulder, and murmured, "Ah, this is a grand place to be." And as I rest in that safe place knowing that my Father is bigger than any storm that beats against the windowpane of my life, I can watch the rains and listen to the thunder, knowing that everything is all right. Here I can feel the beat of my Father's heart.[2]

Our homes are training grounds for faith. By providing a warm and loving environment where our children are free to be vulnerable, honest, and humble—where it is safe to trust—we prepare our children to trust God.

WARMING THEIR HEARTS BY DEMONSTRATING THE FATHER'S LOVE

How our children view God will largely determine their interest in pursuing His presence and plan for their lives. If they perceive Him as impatient, judgmental, and critical, it's unlikely that they will want to get better acquainted. How can we make sure our children form an accurate image of God in their minds?

Again, our children's most enduring beliefs about God are based upon our parenting model. For better or worse, whether we like it or not, we represent God to our kids. The impact of our model upon their long-term memory is especially powerful when they are younger. As toddlers, they look up from their cribs and see an awesome creature—a being who is all-powerful, all-wise. And because they have no choice but to trust him or her, they assume this being to be all-loving. To our children, what we say is true, what we expect is law, how we treat them is love. Because our children so closely associate us with godlikeness, the way we respond to their needs forms the basis of their image of God. It's sobering to note that this first impression is a lasting one.

One lady shared how, after twenty years of being a Christian, she still had trouble disciplining herself to spend time with God in prayer. She'd sit down to pray and read God's Word and immediately become restless and distracted. Something blocked her efforts. Though she knew in her head that God cared for her and wanted to spend time with her, she doubted in her heart that He would ever really be interested. Her earthly father had been so wrapped up in his career that he never showed much interest in the details of her life. She had never really felt close to him. "He was like a shadow—hardly ever home, and when he was, he preferred to be left alone." It was hard for her to believe that God, a parent like her earthly father, would want to spend time with her and that He was concerned about her personal life. Her image of God was distorted because her father modeled a busy and preoccupied God.

We give our children their first taste of God. Depending on how well we represent Him, we will either whet or spoil their appetites. Steve Green, well-known Christian recording artist, recalls how his parents' love stirred his hunger for God.

> ...I have stirring memories of the Lord's presence in our home. When Dad apologized to Mom and, with sincere humility acknowledged a wrong done, I tasted the Lord's goodness and sensed God's presence. When from the heart Mom forgave an obvious injustice, or when, together, Mom and Dad chose to love or give or serve, we children experienced a mysterious joy....
>
> How grateful I am for parents who, through their daily routine of life in simple obedience to the Lord, allowed our home to be permeated with the wonderful sweetness of the Spirit of God.[3]

In sharp contrast, Rick's father left a bitter taste in his mouth for God. Rick's dad believed in running a "tight ship." Infractions met with swift and sometimes cruel punishment. Rick shares,

> The atmosphere at dinner was always tense. We were always afraid we would do something wrong and set Dad off. If we spilled our milk or put our elbows on the table or interrupted someone, Dad would have us stand in front of him and he would strike our foreheads with his dinner fork. It didn't hurt as much as it humiliated us.

As a man in his thirties, Rick explains that when he sins he has difficulty feeling forgiven and walks in condemnation for days.

> Guess I just can't believe God can really love me enough to forgive me. I feel like I still need to be punished. I know in

my head that God is not like my father, but I just can't trust Him to really love me.

Though Rick knows what the Bible says about God's character, the memory of his father's response to his need for forgiveness overrides the truth and prevents him from experiencing God's love and forgiveness on an emotional level. As a child, Rick lacked the discernment to see how his father's attitudes and behavior were an inaccurate reflection of God. Now, as an adult, the distorted image he internalized as a child negatively influences his relationships with God and others.

Because we are the first Bible our children will read, it is crucial for us to truly demonstrate God's love and character. If we portray a grumpy, frustrated, and impatient God, or a preoccupied, busy, and neglectful God, it's unlikely our children will show much interest in seeking Him. On the other hand, if we depict an understanding, kind, and compassionate God, we should expect our children to want to know and serve Him. Paul challenges us to be examples: *"Follow my example, as I follow the example of Christ"* (1 Corinthians 11:1).

If we depict an understanding, kind, and compassionate God, we should expect our children to want to know and serve Him.

How we respond to the needs of our children has a huge bearing on whether or not they fulfill their callings. First, our response affects their ability to trust. Faithful parents are likely to produce faith-filled kids. Our children's capacity to trust is the womb from which God's seed of faith germinates and is born.

Second, consistently meeting our children's needs shapes, to a great degree, our children's understanding of God. If our parent model reflects a God who forgives, protects, and understands, we are likely to pique our children's interest in Him.

For Those from Less than Ideal Homes

What if you grew up in a home where trust was broken and God's love was poorly represented? Is there any hope? Yes, though it's God's perfect will that the parent-child bond provide a context for comprehending His love and character, God can reveal Himself directly to your heart through His Word and Spirit and sovereignly bring forth faith from the seed of His Word. The following Scriptures confirm this idea:

> *I keep asking that the God of our Lord Jesus Christ, the glorious Father, may give you the Spirit of wisdom and revelation, so that you may know him better.*   (Ephesians 1:17)

> *Consequently, faith comes from hearing the message, and the message is heard through the word of Christ.*   (Romans 10:17)

See Appendix E, "Breaking the Cycle Worksheet., for more help for those from less than ideal homes.

PERSONAL INVENTORY

Do your children see the Father in your parenting? Are you building in your child a healthy capacity to trust? The two surveys below are designed to help you determine how well you represent God to your child and where your child's level of trust stands at present.

If your score indicates that trust has been broken, do not despair. Restoring damaged trust when we are to blame normally requires only three things:

1. I am sorry.

2. I was wrong.

3. Please forgive me.

Typically, children are quick to forgive when you humble yourself. Watch out, however, if your child indicates that your apologies are getting old. When hurtful behavior becomes a pattern, it's time to get help.

Kids are resilient. It takes a steady stream of unrepentant and hurtful behavior to scar a child emotionally. The one exception to this is sexual abuse. Even a single incident will require professional help.

You may discover from the results of this inventory that you need to repair your parenting model and restore damaged trust, or you may find that your child's heart is ready to burst into flame with a passion for Jesus. Whether you need to make many adjustments or just a few, the chapters that follow will help you to build and fortify your child's spiritual foundation.

MODELING THE FATHER'S LOVE ASSESSMENT SURVEY

My child would say that I am:

(5) All the time (4) Mostly (3) Sometimes (2) Rarely (1) Never

_____1. Available

_____2. Faithful to keep my promises

_____3. Supportive

_____4. Kind, gentle, and sensitive

_____5. Protective

_____6. Patient

_____7. Generous

_____8. Compassionate and understanding

_____9. Wise

_____10. Just

_____**Subtotal**

My child would say that I am:

(5) Never (4) Rarely (3) Sometimes (2) Mostly (1) All the time

_____1. Harsh

_____2. Unreasonable

_____3. Unforgiving

_____4. Hard to please

_____5. Passive

_____6. Unpredictable

_____7. Aloof and distant

_____8. Condemning

_____9. Selfish

_____10. Angry

_____**Subtotal**

_____**Grand Total (combine subtotals)**

If your *grand total* was between 20 and 40, your child is not getting an accurate picture of God from your parenting model. You may, in this case, need to ask God to help you to grow into His image so that you may more truly reflect His love through your words and behavior. As you yield to God's Spirit and His Word, He is more than able to assist you in this endeavor:

> *Do not conform any longer to the pattern of this world, but be transformed by the renewing of your mind. Then you will be able to test and approve what God's will is—his good, pleasing and perfect will.* (Romans 12:2)

If you scored between 41 and 60, your child sees the likeness of God in your parenting and, with some corrections in your parent model, will develop an accurate understanding of the nature and character of God. If you scored between 61 and 100, your child is currently internalizing an appropriate representation of the Father's love and protection through your care.

TRUST DEVELOPMENT SURVEY

(5) All the time (4) Mostly (3) Sometimes (2) Rarely (1) Never

_____1. My child talks to me about his/her problems.

_____2. If I have hurt my child's feelings, he/she tells me soon after the incident.

_____3. My child likes to please me.

_____4. When my child is overwhelmed, he/she asks me for help.

_____5. My child shares with me opinions and interests about which he/she knows I am uncomfortable.

_____6. My child shares his/her failures with me and seeks my consolation.

_____7. My child is openly affectionate with me. (Boys may demonstrate this by roughhousing.)

_____8. My child confesses and seeks my forgiveness when he/she has done something wrong.

_____9. My child asks me to do fun things with him/her.

_____10. My child talks to me about his/her friends.

_____**Subtotal**

(5) Never (4) Rarely (3) Sometimes (2) Mostly (1) All the time

_____1. My child tends to hide his/her emotions.

_____2. When I correct my child, he/she defies me by tuning me out and shrugging off my instruction, or by talking back and arguing with me.

_____3. My child is easily disappointed.

_____4. My child is cynical and sarcastic.

_____5. My child pushes me away when I am affectionate.

_____6. My child is withdrawn and sullen around me.

_____7. My child is uncomfortable when I compliment him/her—sometimes contradicting what I have said.

_____8. My child becomes nervous and uncomfortable when I visit his/her room.

_____9. My child flinches when I raise my hand.

_____10. My child bends the truth and sometimes lies to me.

_____Subtotal

_____Grand total (combine subtotals)

If your *grand total* was between 20 and 40, your child is tentative about his or her relationship with you. You may, in this case, want to consider how you can restore your child's confidence; some suggestions follow. If you scored between 41 and 60, your child is growing in trust and, with some adjustments on your part, will develop a healthy capacity to express faith. If your child scored between 61 and 100, your child is comfortable depending on you and has a vigorous ability to trust.

<u>Chapter Notes</u>

1. Gloria Gaither, *What My Parents Did Right!* (West Monroe, La.: Howard Publishing Co., Inc., 2002), 8–9.
2. Jill Briscoe, "In the Father's Arms" (sermon, *Preaching Today Audio Series*, tape no. 141). For more information, please refer to www.PreachingToday.com or www.PreachingTodayAudio.com.
3. Gloria Gaither, *What My Parents Did Right!*, 130.

CHAPTER 6

Protection:
The First Emotional Need

Meeting our children's emotional needs lays a foundation for destiny. Our children develop a healthy capacity to trust and an accurate image of God when we satisfy the yearning of their souls. They are ready and willing to depend on God; they know of His kind and tender ways because they have seen Him in us.

A child has seven emotional needs. These needs form the acrostic PARENTS. They are:

> Protection,
>
> Acceptance,
>
> Recognition,
>
> Enforced Limits,
>
> Nearness,
>
> Time, and
>
> Support.

PROTECTION

A she-wolf locates her den near the top of a high hill, where predators can be easily spotted and defended against. She digs her den with one opening so that she and her mate may guard the door at all times, allowing nothing in or out without their consent. Inside, up to five pups find warmth and sustenance against her body. Wolf parents go to great lengths to provide a safe and well-protected den. Your children need a safe and well-protected home to grow up in as well. They need a place where they can rest and be cared for—a refuge where the ugly unfairness of life is kept at bay, where emotional and physical threat is arrested at the door, and where warmth and nourishment are provided inside.

Trust flourishes in homes where children know they can run into their mom or dad's arms at any moment and find love and protection. Children who feel safe are free to let down their defenses and let their parents care for them. They view trust as a positive experience and an effective way of meeting their needs.

Rather than resort to unhealthy patterns of self-protection to manage fear (denial, procrastination, defensiveness, and explosive anger), these children trust others and God (the ultimate parent) to help them manage their needs. As adults, when faced with fear-provoking circumstances, they exercise trust and seek help from God and others. Just as they chose to run into their parents' arms for reassurance when they were children, they now choose to run into the arms of their Father in heaven.

Kim, a woman in her forties, shares,

My father's hugs were able to take away any fear I ever had when I was a child. I would run to him and bury my head in his chest, and he would hold me tight for a long time. During those moments, all my fears melted away. Now, I'm an adult, when I am afraid, I imagine God, my heavenly Father, giving me a hug just like my father used to. It really helps to ease my fears.

Chaz, a father of three, shares,

We had rabbits when I was a child. A neighborhood bully visited our backyard once and began to terrorize them. I was only six and watched in horror as the boy picked up one of the rabbits by an ear. My father, looking out from the kitchen window, came running out the back door and removed the boy from the yard. I'll never forget how safe I felt at that moment. Like my father, I know God is watching out for me and will take care of me when the bullies of life threaten to harm me or those I love.

Let's take a closer look at the characteristics of a safe home. Children feel safe in environments where the relationships they depend upon are stable and predictable. The status of the marriage relationship is a matter of particular importance to a child. If marital conflict dominates the emotional landscape of the home for an extended period of time, a child is overwhelmed by a preeminent concern: "Who will take care of me?" Adding to this distress, a child may feel compelled to take sides in the marriage. Siding with one parent against the other often leaves a child devastated by guilt as he considers how he has betrayed the loyalty of a mother or father. Finally, a child is often so desperate to see the marriage restored that he takes responsibility for trying to fix it and assumes the role of mediator. He is likely to assume responsibility for the demise of the relationship as well, and morbidly seek to discover his part in its failure. A forty-year-old father, raised by parents who were in constant conflict, relates,

My parents' turbulent marriage really disturbed me as a child. I was always waiting for the shoe to drop. Mom would threaten Dad with divorce, and I just knew that it was a matter of time. Somehow, they managed to stay together, but I find I have a lot of fear and insecurities as a result.

Protection: The First Emotional Need

In order to feel safe, children need their parents to work hard at resolving their differences peacefully, fairly, and in a timely manner. They need them to get whatever help is necessary to maintain their marriage commitment and to build a more harmonious home. Some conflict is to be expected in marriage. It's how it is handled that makes or breaks a child's future. When differences are managed honestly and responsibly, children grow up unscathed and equipped with excellent relational skills.

When divorce has occurred or is pending, parents can limit the emotional fallout their child may suffer by putting the child's needs first. As much as possible, couples should set aside their differences and seek what is best for the child by letting him know that it's okay to love both of them and by not forcing him to take sides. Though you may not need your spouse, your child needs his parent. A child needs his mom and his dad.

Children feel secure when parents acknowledge and value their needs and feelings.

Parents should also talk about the divorce early and regularly so their child has time to adjust and prepare for the loss of a mother or father from his home. Divorce, it has been said, is like a death that doesn't die—a parent is gone but not completely. Children need time (years) to grieve what they lost through divorce. Parents can help by understanding the stages of grief and by patiently helping their children through feelings of denial, disappointment, anger, and hopelessness. In light of the devastating effects of divorce upon children, it's understandable why God says He hates it in Malachi 2:16.

Another characteristic of a safe home is respect. Children feel secure when parents acknowledge and value their needs and feelings. In homes that are safe, being in need is not a shameful thing. Needs for affection, comfort, and recognition are treated with the utmost dignity—they are not overlooked or minimized. When children are afraid, for instance, parents acknowledge their fear and do not belittle it or overreact. They patiently explain the fear-causing situation and teach that God is in control by modeling prayer and sharing Bible stories.

Parents who fail to honor and respect their children's needs and feelings promote the belief that being in need and asking for help is a sign of weakness and deficiency. The mother, for instance, who sighs in despair as she cleans up the bed sheets, "Why do you have to be so needy," causes her child to feel deficient about his need for greater bladder control. Likewise, the father who berates his son, "Stop acting like a baby," when he cries, encourages his son to drive his need for help underground. Children from homes like these view legitimate needs as shameful. They grow up despising their vulnerability and unwilling to acknowledge their need for help. Chris, an electrician in his late thirties, was raised in a home where it was not okay to be in need. Today, he battles depression partly because he holds himself in ferocious self-contempt whenever he is in need.

> I hate feeling weak, helpless, and needy. I believe I should be able to take care of myself and feel worthless and angry when I can't. My counselor asked me if I could remember a time when my parents comforted me when I was in need. I couldn't think of one time. I just remember being told to grow up and to not be such a pain.

Chris's depression finds much of its power in his self-contempt. For years he struggled with underlying feelings of helplessness and despair but was unwilling to accept the fact that he needed help. Now, even in the midst of a full-blown depression, he still resists the truth about his vulnerable and dependent condition. He is terrified to admit he might have a need he cannot manage on his own and despises himself for it. Because he felt unable to trust his parents to meet his needs, he fears reaching out for help and being hurt and disappointed again. He struggles to believe that anyone, including God, is really willing and able to help him. Alone in his pain, he hates himself for being weak and worthless.

In contrast, children from homes that recognize and respect needs and feelings are open and honest about their need for help. They are free to express their vulnerability without shame and to communicate their needs openly: "Daddy, I'm feeling sad; will you hug me?" and, "Mom, it hurt my feelings when you said that." As adults, they are able to admit their needs and entrust them to others. In terms of their relationship with God, they express themselves fully to God and boldly trust Him with their needs. They are fully able to *approach the throne of grace with confidence, so that* [they] *may receive mercy and find grace to help* [them] *in* [their] *time of need"* (Hebrews 4:16).

Children who grow up feeling well protected and cared for are not compelled to manage their needs in their own strength.

Protecting our children also means screening harmful media and peer influences that might undermine their callings. Unchecked, a deluge of popular culture can convince a child that "everybody's doing it," virgins are geeks, and that violence is the way to solve any dispute. Though our kids may not always agree with our opinions on what is acceptable TV or music entertainment, if handled correctly, they can't miss our motivation. A teen boy shares, "It drives me crazy when my mom turns off shows that I want to watch, but I know she is not doing it to be mean. She cares for me and wants to protect me." Children must be trained to discern fact from fiction. Until they are spiritually mature enough to see through the lies disseminated through the media and strong enough to resist their seductive force, parents must guard the door against the distortions of popular culture.

Parents willing to make hard calls for the sake of their children's spiritual growth model God's passion for purity and holiness. By controlling the flow of media messages into our homes and monitoring our children's peer relationships, we instill in our children an understanding that God values clean minds and clean hearts.

Blessed are the pure in heart, for they will see God.
(Matthew 5:8)

As parents supervise media and peer influences, they must be careful not to "overprotect" their children. Children need to learn how to think for themselves. When parents make all the decisions in the home, children come to believe that they are incapable of making wise choices. They believe that something must be wrong with them since their parents place so little trust in them. Overprotecting a child can hinder a child's calling as much as being too permissive—both undermine self-confidence and damage trust.

Finally, a safe home protects children from each another. The truth is, names as well as sticks and stones can hurt a child and leave him with permanent scars. In well-protected homes, ridicule, cruel sarcasm, and name-calling—as well as sticks and stones—are forbidden. Our kids need us to intervene with firm limits and discipline when disagreements between siblings get out of control. Conflict comes naturally to children, but conflict resolution does not; it must be modeled and taught.

Children who grow up feeling well protected and cared for are not compelled to manage their needs in their own strength. They don't need to resort to manipulation and control; instead, they honestly admit their needs and trust others, especially God, to meet them. Their willingness to receive makes them candidates for the grace and provision of God, who *"gives grace to the humble"* (James 4:6) but resists the proud.

In addition, as parents satisfy their children's need for protection, they model the goodness and strength of God. These children grow up with an understanding that God, like their parents, is in control and has their best interests in mind. They are, therefore, inclined to trust His plan for their lives and depend on His strength to achieve it.

ACTION QUESTIONS

1. Are the relationships in your home (especially your marriage) stable and harmonious? If not, what can you do to get help?

2. What are you doing to improve the quality of your marriage?

3. If divorce has occurred (or is pending), how have you assured your child that he/she is safe and loved?

4. Do you respect your child by listening to his/her feelings and acknowledging his/her needs?

5. Do you become impatient and irritated when your child is afraid or angry, or do you try to understand what he/she is feeling?

6. Do you protect your child from misleading media messages that can potentially influence his/her perception of himself/herself and the world? Do you limit the flow of media into your home and help your child to accurately interpret media messages?

7. Do you know your child's friends? Are you aware of their values and the condition of their home lives? Do you monitor the influence they have on your child? Do you get to know your child's friends before you permit him/her to go to their houses or to an event with them?

8. Do you intervene when your child is being treated unfairly in a sibling conflict? Do your children feel protected from one another?

CHAPTER 7

Acceptance:
The Second Emotional Need

When my daughter, Rachael, was four she asked me in tears, "Do you think I'm pretty, Daddy?"

"Of course," I said. "Why do you ask?"

"Well, when I look in the mirror, my cheeks are not as skinny as Barbie's."

I was heartbroken. My daughter was a preschooler, and she was already comparing herself to Hollywood's unrealistic standards of beauty.

Rachael needed to know that I accepted her no matter what the standards of the world might say. Looking into her big, brown, tear-filled eyes I said, "Rachael, you are absolutely beautiful. Barbie means nothing to me. I love you just the way you are."

Children crave acceptance. They crave it from their peers, from their teachers and coaches, and, most importantly, they crave it from you, their parents. They need to know that despite natural limitations, physical imperfections, and poor performance, they are still worthy of your love.

If this need goes unmet, a child's calling is jeopardized in two ways. First, an absence of acceptance negatively affects the child's view of herself. Feelings of inferiority are commonly responsible for self-sabotaging behaviors that often undercut a child's pursuit of God's plan. A child who feels like an "idiot," for instance, will work toward proving his theory correct. Second, a lack of acceptance from parents is likely to cause a child's perception of God to be distorted. Again, a child who has an incorrect understanding of God and His ways will have a difficult time trusting and receiving from Him.

Our response to our children's needs is the primary source of their self-perception. We are the first mirror into which our children will gaze. If our children don't perceive our acceptance, they are likely to internalize a belief that they are unacceptable.

We are also the main source of our children's perception of God. As discussed in a previous chapter, children transfer our responses to their needs to God—a parent figure. If we regularly criticize and shame our children, they are likely to develop a belief that God is condemning and difficult to please.

☙☙☙☙

Although Sue was an attractive and intelligent child, her mother regularly reminded her that she was not living up to her potential. Throughout her childhood, Sue was subjected to relentless criticism and comparison to her peer's physical appearance and social graces. Sue tried to win her mother's approval, but it was always out of reach. Eventually Sue internalized her mother's lack of acceptance and today feels flawed and inadequate. In addition, Sue interpreted her mother's response to her needs as God's response. Though she professes that God loves her, she doubts, on an emotional level, that God really accepts her the way she is. She struggles with opening up to God and giving herself fully to Him for fear of His condemnation and judgment.

The effects of Sue's negative feelings about herself and her distorted perceptions of God are far reaching. They affect her parenting, her marriage, and the calling God has on her life. Sue's self-contempt makes her irritable, easily frustrated, and defensive. Her children complain of her nasty temper. Her husband reports that she is often angry and difficult to get along with. Her belief that God doesn't love her completely keeps her from fully embracing His plan for her life. She holds back from God and remains distant and suspicious. At one point, she believed that if she completely gave her life to God, He would send her to a far off and treacherous country to serve as a missionary.

Our response to our children's needs is the primary source of their self-perception.

Sue's view of herself and her God are distorted because the mirrors through which she saw herself and God when she was a child were broken. Shattered mirrors, shattered images. Because Sue's parents were unable to meet her need for acceptance, she believed that she was unacceptable and unworthy of love—even God's love. If Sue does not get the help she needs to overcome the negative feelings she has about herself and about her God, she will pass them on to her children just as her mother did to her.

A lack of acceptance disables our children in other ways as well. In families that lack acceptance, children (and parents) are likely to feel they are loved only when they do the right thing. In these homes, acceptance is given only to children when parental expectations are fulfilled. It is offered conditionally and based upon performance. The effects of conditional love are devastating: Children grow up feeling like they must earn the love of God and others.

When George did well in school, his parents lavished him with affection and attention. When he performed poorly, he met harsh criticism from his father and icy silence from his mother. "It was almost like my dad and mom took my performance personally," George reflected. "If I wasn't being successful, it offended them."

As a child, George construed his parents behavior to mean: "You are not worthy of love unless you meet certain standards of achievement." Out of this experience, he formed a concept of love and acceptance that was defined by performance: Love and acceptance are earned through accomplishment. Today, George (a corporate executive) is driven to achieve. When he is unproductive, he feels miserable. (He feels unacceptable and unloved.) When he succeeds, he is euphoric. (He regards himself as acceptable and worthy of love.) His week is a cycle of intense emotional highs and lows. At the end of a day, he is exhausted from his efforts to sustain himself emotionally and returns home with nothing left to give his wife and children. God help George if he is ever unemployed.

George's relationship with God is directly affected by this concept of love. Because George believes that love is earned, his relationship with God is based on works. George only feels loved by God when he is serving

Recognize and appreciate your children's unique gifts and interests while avoiding negative comparisons with others.

Him in some capacity. Though he holds many positions at church, he is quick to judge himself and others for "not doing enough for God." His devotional life, though well disciplined, is void of intimacy. George sees God as a taskmaster who is never really pleased with him and continually expects him to do more and more. He perceives the love he receives from God the same way he received love as a child.

Many of us have good biblical theology and doctrine, but precious little of it is reflected in daily life. We know God loves us unconditionally—He loves us regardless of our performance—yet we run ourselves ragged trying to earn His favor and beat ourselves up emotionally for falling short of His expectations. Like George, we are far more influenced by the concept of God we inherited from our parents than by our conscious understanding of biblical doctrine.

One other damaging effect of a lack of acceptance is worth mentioning. When older children do not find the acceptance they need at home, they will seek it elsewhere. Josh McDowell, youth specialist and author, quoted a study that stated that, among teens who were sexually active, 58 percent felt they had never gotten to know their fathers and 40 percent had never gotten to know their mothers.[1] Children who suffer from an empty emotional tank will often turn to their peers to fill it.

⌖⌖⌖⌖

Sheila's father was home most nights, but this was not much comfort to the rest of the family. His law practice was stressful and demanding, and he spent most nights channel surfing. When he did relate to family members, he was usually impatient and critical. It wasn't long after Sheila became a teen that she began to meet her need for love through promiscuous relationships.

Though God is willing to fill the void in young people's lives, those who feel unloved by their parents are often unable to receive it. They may believe God loves them, but on a heartfelt level assume that, like their parents, He loves them conditionally and at some point will reject them. Fearful of being disappointed and hurt again, they resist His love and, taking matters into their own hands, look for love in all the wrong places.

⌖⌖⌖⌖

Rudy was eight when his father left his mother for another woman. Like many elementary-aged children who experience the loss of a parent to divorce, Rudy interpreted his father's departure as personal rejection.

It was like my dad suddenly died in a car accident. He never acknowledged me on my birthday, holidays, or any special events. But if he had died it would have been easier to handle. Because he lived across town, I constantly wondered why he didn't love me enough to stay.

As a teen, Rudy filled the absence of his father's love with sex and drugs. Promiscuous sex offered him a way to connect with another human being without becoming vulnerable. Drugs promised to numb the pain of rejection. Even after Rudy came to Christ, he struggled with these life-controlling problems. Though God reached out His arms to embrace him, Rudy had difficulty believing that God could love him any differently than he had previously been loved. Alone, hurting, and unable to experience the reality of God's love, Rudy continued to abuse drugs and view pornography to medicate his pain.

What can we do to create an atmosphere of unconditional acceptance in our homes? First, we recognize and appreciate our children's unique gifts, personalities, and interests. This means we discontinue all comparisons with siblings, friends, or relatives immediately. A child needs to know that our love is not graded on a curve. He needs to know that we love him for being him—for his special abilities, personality, and interests. Middle children are especially prone to believe our love is partial. We might want to reassure them, "You are special. We love you each the same amount but each in a special way." Affirming our children as individuals lets them know that they are wonderful and lovable just the way God made them.

Accepting our children also means we focus on behavior, not the person, when we discipline. Exploding in anger or harshly criticizing a child when he disappoints us sends a painful message of rejection. Increased volume, incidentally, does not ensure increased responsiveness. Often the opposite is true. Yelling breeds resentment and reduces cooperation. *"Speaking the truth in love"* (Ephesians 4:15), as the Bible suggests, puts the child's feelings first and offers correction without personal attack. If a child refuses to cooperate with your requests, switch to a calmly stated command: "I want you to pick up your clothes now." Follow up with consequences that do not humiliate. Rules, by the way, should be realistic and not too rigid or too flexible. Our goal is to create a compassionate and secure atmosphere where kids feel safe and appreciated.

It's important to learn mature and productive ways to manage our anger if we are to avoid wounding our children. Venting our frustrations upon our kids is selfish and cruel and will ultimately destroy the bond of trust between us.

Another way to meet our children's need for acceptance is to listen to their words and feelings. Children have a profound need to be understood—we all do. We crush our children when our motive for listening is simply to gain enough information to defeat their arguments or change their opinions. When a child complains about a math problem, a response like, "Oh, come on! It's not that hard," minimizes her feelings. She feels humiliated by that reply. A more understanding response would be, "That's not easy, is it? But I've seen you handle a problem like this before." She needs us to listen to her feelings, not her words. If our child timidly reports that she has gotten into trouble in Sunday school, instead of "What did you do now?" a better reply might be, "Its sounds like you had a tough time. Tell me what happened." Listening in order to understand our children's feelings communicates our interest in them as individuals with unique feelings and needs.

> *Children have a profound need to be understood—we all do.*

Listening to our children's words and feelings is not easy when what they have to say threatens us. If they say, "I hate school!" we may be tempted to play down or reject their feelings—especially if we home school! Nevertheless, we undercut any possibility of helping our children to change their beliefs if we fail to understand their feelings first. Until we can honestly say, "Wow. I think I understand what you are going through. No wonder you feel that way," our advice will only serve to damage our children's trust and make them feel worse.

As a general rule, don't share your opinion until you have told your child to his satisfaction what you hear him saying. Reflecting back to your child what you think you hear him saying lets him know you understand. For example, when our daughter tells us that she was not invited to a party, we might respond, "I hate the feeling of being left out by others. Is that what you are feeling?" To be understood is to be known. It is to be accepted, affirmed, and respected as a unique individual with a distinct point of view.

Acknowledging our child's negative feelings does not mean we tolerate negative behavior. Inappropriate behavior is inappropriate and should be treated as such. A child's feelings and a child's behavior are two separate entities and must be addressed separately.

To promote an atmosphere of acceptance in your home, when differences arise, learn to disagree agreeably. Speak respectfully to your children when you clash. Rather than ordering your kids around, speak politely, "Please pick up your room." Ban put-downs, vicious sarcasm, and disrespectful gestures. Forgive each other completely and without "ifs," "ands," or "buts" before resentment builds.

Be prepared to help your children work through the inevitable self-doubts that will crash in upon their lives.

Finally, to help your children feel accepted, you should be prepared to help them work through the inevitable self-doubts that will crash in upon their lives. Let them know that God has a special plan for their lives—a plan that takes into account their limitations.

Phil, a bright and confident seminarian, bore a red birthmark that ran down his forehead and nose and across a large section of his mouth and neck. It looked like a horrible burn scar. Yet the promising minister oozed self-assurance and a positive attitude toward life. A friend of his gathered up the courage to ask him how he was able to overcome his handicap.

> "Because of my dad," he said. "My dad taught me, as far back as I can remember, that this part of my face was where an angel kissed me before I was even born. He said to me, 'Son, this mark was for your dad, so that I might know that you are mine. You have been marked out by God just to remind me that you're my son.' All through my youth, as I grew up, I was reminded by my dad, 'You are the most important, special fellow on the earth.'"

> He ended with this astounding statement: "To tell you the truth, I got to where I felt sorry for people who didn't have birth marks across the sides of their faces!"

As a child feels the unconditional acceptance of his parents, he becomes increasingly convinced that, despite his natural limitations and physical imperfections, God loves him and has a wonderful plan for his life. Because his parents love him just the way he is, he is confident his heavenly Parent does as well. As an adult, he senses God's support as he reaches out in pursuit of his calling. He knows that he doesn't need to depart from the way he is to go to find the love he needs. He looks no farther than his prayer closet to experience the love and acceptance his soul craves.

ACTION QUESTIONS

1. Are there certain things about your child (personality quirks or physical characteristics) that, as much as you hate to admit it, really bother you? Why do these things annoy you? Who can you talk to about it?

2. When you are frustrated, do you tend to take it out on your child? What safeguards can you put in place to stop spillover anger?

3. Can you see how your child is truly unique and special? What qualities make him/her one of a kind? What can you do to help your child see his/her unique giftedness, personality, and interests today? How can you call attention to them?

4. Are you careful not to shame your child (make him/her feel bad about himself/herself) when you discipline him/her? Do you separate your child's behavior from his/her person? Do you speak respectfully to your child? Do you order your child around, or do you state your requests politely?

5. Do you compare your child with others?

6. Do you listen to your child's words and feelings? Do you try to understand what is going on inside him/her emotionally? Do you try to see things from his/her point of view?

7. Does your child feel comfortable talking to you about his/her limitations, failures, and fears? This is a good indication of how accepted your child feels by you.

8. Do you become impatient with your child's performance? Does he/she easily frustrate you? Is he/she too slow? Sloppy? Loud? Rash? Disobedient? How can you change your perception of your child so that his/her behavior is less irritating? How can you better manage your frustration and anger?

9. Are you ashamed of certain aspects of your child's performance, appearance, and personality? What can you do to change this? Who can you talk to?

10. Are your expectations for his/her performance realistic?

Chapter Notes

1. Mike Yorkey, gen. ed., *Growing a Healthy Home* (Brentwood, Tenn.: Wolgemuth & Hyatt, 1990), 207.

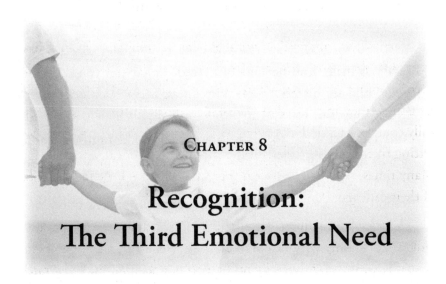

CHAPTER 8

Recognition:
The Third Emotional Need

I asked a teen boy who had been caught vandalizing a gym locker what would cause him to act this way. His immediate and insightful answer took me back. "Since I can't please my father by doing right, I might as well do wrong!"

It crushes a child to feel like a failure in his parent's eyes. Your children have an intense desire to please you. They need to hear you say, "I'm proud of you. Good job. I respect you." They need to feel your approval.

Even Jesus was recognized by His Father. During His baptism—before He had performed one miracle or given a single sermon—a voice thundered from heaven, *"This is my Son, whom I love; with him I am well pleased"* (Matthew 3:17).

Children from homes that are high on expectation and low on affirmation commonly grow up with a nagging sense of inadequacy. Since they could not win their parents' approval, they are convinced that they are deficient and "not good enough." They may resort to people pleasing to cancel out these feelings or they may try to prove themselves "good enough" through their careers and ministry performance.

Sometimes, approval is withheld for so long that a child loses hope. Children who seek in vain to win their parents' approval may become so hurt and disappointed that they give up trying to achieve. As adults, they may avoid responsibility and seem unable to successfully complete a task. Underlying their behavior is the fear that they are setting themselves up for painful criticism, disapproval, and rejection. Many times, such people retreat into unproductive lives and fall short of their callings.

A lack of recognition from parents has debilitating effects on a child's relationship with God as well. Since a child's perception of God is, to a large extent, formed by his parents' model, the child who rarely feels his parents' approval grows up with the belief that God cannot be pleased. God becomes something of a tyrant in his mind—merciless, exacting, and severe.

> Children who rarely feel their parents' approval grow up with the belief that God cannot be pleased. They need to hear you say, "I'm proud of you. Good job. I respect you."

Greg's father was an unhappy man who felt trapped in his career as a public school-teacher. He vowed his children would go farther than he had in life and demanded high standards from his children, ruthlessly criticizing them when they fell short.

Greg never felt like he was good enough to get his father's approval, but that didn't stop him from trying. He went to the college his father suggested. He routinely called home to report on his corporate career, and he insisted that his wife agree to spend the majority of his vacation time visiting his out-of-state parents. Greg was driven to gain his father's recognition.

In a similar way, Greg was driven to gain the approval of his heavenly Father. Most of the time, he felt guilty for not doing enough for

God, even though he was extremely active in the church. It always seemed to Greg that though God loved him, God didn't really like him. To get God's endorsement, he believed, he would have to work much harder. Children raised by critical parents view God as never being satisfied with their performance and demanding more and more sacrifice. The Bible tells us this is not the character of God. *"But you, O Lord, are a compassionate and gracious God, slow to anger, abounding in love and faithfulness"* (Psalm 86:15).

Those who grew up feeling like they never measured up to their parents' standards likewise commonly find it difficult to believe that God approves of them. Since they were unable to gain their parents' approval, they are sure that they are too deficient and flawed for God's approval. Some conclude that their efforts to please God are futile. They become disillusioned and stop trying. Others never stop climbing the ladder of performance in hopes of finding God's favor at the top. The latter find only temporary relief in their good deeds and frantic activity, however. Because they believe they are not good enough and that God demands more and better service, their striving never ends.

> We are to bring children up in the instruction of the Lord, not offer them up as a kind of child sacrifice.

A gifted musician and charming Christian woman in her thirties, Kylie is a bustle of activity for Jesus. She writes songs, leads worship groups, and records music. Though many would say that she is full of zeal for the Lord, her family reports otherwise. They note that she is frequently "just not around." Growing up in a harsh atmosphere, filled with criticism and void of affirmation, Kylie is starving for recognition. Moving from stage to stage, she desperately seeks the appreciation she never received as a child.

From time to time I will ask an overly committed pastor, "How do your children feel about your long hours of service to the Lord?" The following response is what I hear all too often: "I think they understand. I tell them, 'Your Daddy needs to sacrifice for the Lord.'"

If I recall, it was Molech, the god of the Ammonites who required child sacrifice, not Yahweh. The God of the Bible commands fathers to *"bring* [children] *up in the training and instruction of the Lord"* (Ephesians 6:4)—bring them up, not offer them up. Many ministers and other professional people-helpers (nurses, social workers, counselors) are unaware that they are driven by unmet needs for recognition.

As mentioned earlier, a lack of recognition in childhood can also cause an adult to withdraw from the arena of performance. Donna (late thirties), for instance, never seems to be able to accomplish anything. She has all sorts of unfinished projects and plans but never seems to be able to follow through and complete them. Though she has high hopes for success, she avoids serious goal setting and dedicated effort. She lives in a state of constant distraction and frustration.

For those of us who seek approval from others, life becomes a proving ground.

Donna grew up in a home that withheld praise. It seemed as if her mother had a special knack for evaluating Donna's performance in seconds and finding the one thing that was not done right. If Donna dusted the living room, her mother noticed how the molding still had dust on it. If Donna bought a new outfit, her mother pointed out how it was tight in the hips.

As an adult, Donna avoids activities that can be evaluated and measured. Goal setting and performance are not safe experiences. In Donna's mind, they mean more disappointment, disapproval, and rejection.

For those of us who seek approval from others, life is a proving ground. We engage in herculean efforts and time-consuming projects that steal us away from our families and our Lord in order to refute the nagging doubt that, unless we make a name for ourselves, we will forever go unappreciated and unrecognized. Such is the pathology of workaholism and people pleasing: managing our need for recognition by employing habitual behaviors that seek a constant stream of recognition through performance. On the other hand, some of us were so disappointed in our attempts to please our parents that we simply quit trying. The expectations of others, including the opportunities God has for us, threaten us—they mean more criticism and rejection. We are paralyzed by the prospect of failure and avoid goals and any activity that may be evaluated at all costs.

Yet the Bible shares that God is not hard to please and His response to our obedience is nothing short of full and complete approval:

Well done, good and faithful servant! You have been faithful with a few things; I will put you in charge of many things. Come and share your master's happiness! (Matthew 25:21)

You and I can make God happy. It is not an impossible task; our smallest step of obedience makes Him swell with pride. Even our repentance (and we can all do this) thrills Him with delight. Just as the prodigal son delighted his father with his choice to return home, we can make our heavenly Father proud of us by humbling ourselves and returning to Him.

But we had to celebrate and be glad, because this brother of yours was dead and is alive again; he was lost and is found.
(Luke 15:32)

Paul wrote that we should not *"embitter"* our children, or *"they will become discouraged"* (Colossians 3:21). When we see only what our children do wrong instead of what they do right, we embitter them and discourage them from trying to please us. It's time we caught our children doing something right for a change. Here are five practical suggestions that show you how to praise your children.

1. **Look for the specific good.** Find something worth praising. If your son blows only one right note in his trumpet recital, let him know how good that right note sounded. If your daughter comes in last during a swim competition, let her know she beat her best time. Look for progress, not perfection. Finding the good in our children may seem awkward at first. It may require a conscious effort until it becomes a habit.

2. **Speak the good.** Don't worry; your child will not become prideful as a result of your praise. Research shows it takes ten compliments to balance the negative emotional impact of one criticism—few of us need to worry about our children getting out of balance! You can't overdo it if affirmation is sincere. As your affirming responses begin to outweigh and outnumber the critical ones, incidentally, the atmosphere in your home will begin to change—you will find a more positive and inspirational climate.

3. **Be genuine.** Be enthusiastic and sincere in your praise. Let it flow from your heart. Flattery is manipulative and seeks selfish ends. Praise seeks to build up the recipient. Try compliments such as these: "I'm really impressed!" "That's a home run!" "I knew you were good, but this is better than good." "Can I show this around to others?"

4. **Put a ban on cuts and put-downs, and strictly enforce it.** Make your home a rejection-free environment.

5. **Focus on character.** Compliments attach value to something. If praise concentrates mainly on a child's physical appearance, "You are so pretty," or "You're getting so tall," this indicates that looking good is what is most important in life. Observing acts of kindness and responsibility and applauding attitudes of thankfulness and cooperation shift the spotlight to character and attitude.

What gets rewarded gets repeated. Praise is a powerful tool for developing character qualities in your child. Make a big deal about small things, like a kind word to a sibling, a clean bedroom floor, and chores performed without complaint. By recognizing virtuous behaviors, we are likely to see more of them! See Appendix F, "Service Projects and Chart," to learn how you can turn chores into a source of recognition and service.

Children have a fundamental need to be appreciated. They long to know that we not only accept them, but also approve of them. Our kids need to know that we think they are great! Affirming their abilities and initiative and praising them for jobs well done satisfies their need for recognition and sets them on course to please God. More praise and less criticism is key to raising your children to fulfill their purposes.

ACTION QUESTIONS

1. Have you caught your child doing something right lately? Has your child been kind, grateful, polite, respectful, helpful, responsible, cheerful, neat, or cooperative recently? When was the last time you complimented your child? What was it for?

2. Is your home a training ground where children are free to learn and make mistakes, or a proving ground where their worth hangs in the balance with every job?

3. Do you allow your child to be a child? Is he/she free to make mistakes and learn?

4. Do you criticize more than praise?

5. Keeping in mind that your child is still a child, how realistic are your standards for chores, school projects, and athletic events?

6. Do you typically notice the dust on the molding or your child's willingness to dust?

7. Do you find it hard to praise your child? Are you stingy with compliments? Why do you think that is?

8. Do you want progress or perfection in your child?

9. Do you have strict limits against hurtful words within your home?

10. What one thing can you compliment your child for today? When will you share it with him/her?

CHAPTER 9

Enforced Limits:
The Fourth Emotional Need

Ken was afraid to say no to his son. Though he was a strapping man of over six feet, a big game hunter, and a former construction worker, he was afraid that he would lose his son's love if he stood up to him and enforced the rules of his home. Sadly, Ken's greatest fear came true: As a teen, his son rejected him for being weak and withdrew behind a wall of sullen silence.

In the absence of rules and limits, a child feels insecure. Do you remember how you felt in grade school when there was no adult supervision on the playground? Remember the bullies? Remember your frustration as the rules of the kickball game were ignored or kept changing? Children need rules and limits to feel protected.

Behavioral problems, in fact, are often a way a child asks for help. A child who feels anxious "acts out" his need for someone to bring structure and safety into his life. In a sense, a child really does "ask for it." Have you noticed how your little ones act up when you are on the phone? They are feeling anxious. They miss your focused attention. Or how about your teen who has a big test the next day? Her irritability is a product of her anxiety. It's a cry for help. Firm guidance and boundaries demonstrate our willingness to help our children find the control they seek. Without loving discipline, children feel a lack of protection and care. They are even prone to feel resentment toward their parents for its absence, as in the case of Ken's son. Kids want parents they can respect and trust. They need parents, not pals.

The book of Proverbs frequently refers to a child's need for discipline. Proverbs 19:18 even says that to allow a child's selfish will to go unchecked is to act as an accomplice to his death: *"Discipline your son, for in that there is hope; do not be a willing party to his death."* In effect, parents impose a sentence of death upon their children if they do not enforce their limits.

A forty-year-old man who had just been released from drug rehab candidly shared with me his grief over the lack of discipline he received as a child. "I never knew what it felt like to have my stubborn will broken until I lost my job and was locked up in a treatment center with drug dealers and gang members from some of the roughest cities in the nation." This man came close to death because he had never learned to yield his will. What he could have learned by the age of four took him much of his life to discover.

> *Parents who do not consistently enforce limits instill in their children a false understanding of God and the universe He created.*

A child's response to authority is shaped, to a large extent, by a parent's response to his need for limits. For instance, a child who was raised in an environment where "No" means "Maybe you can talk me out of it," or "Yes, if you wear me down," is likely, when he is an adult, to have difficulty accepting God's Word as the final word on standards of conduct and doctrine. Since he was able to successfully resist his parent's will, he is apt, as a grown-up, to oppose God's will or manipulate His Word to get his own way.

Surrendering to our children's demands is not only cowardly, but it's also cruel. If "No" means "Maybe" when our children are young, why should it mean anything different when they are old?

Parents who do not consistently enforce limits instill in their children a false understanding of God and the universe He created. When God says, "Thou shalt not," He means it. Whining will do no good—His Word cannot be changed. *"Not the smallest letter, not the least stroke of a pen, will by any means disappear from the Law until everything is accomplished"* (Matthew 5:18). Demanding our own way serves no purpose other than to make us frustrated, angry, and depressed. The reality is: What God says, God means—it cannot be altered to accommodate personal interest, *"The word of the Lord stands forever"* (1 Peter 1:25).

Not only is God's Word timeless truth, it is also binding law. When God's law is broken, consequences inevitably follow—and many times, they are painful.

Children from homes that fail to enforce limits often have difficulty appreciating the fact that *"the wages of sin is death"* (Romans 6:23). They are inclined to believe that the price tag for sin is not real. Sadly, this will not stop them from getting AIDS, breaking up their families as a result of infidelity, or becoming addicts. Whether a person acknowledges God's law or not doesn't matter—it's Law. *"If you do not obey the Lord your God and do not carefully follow all his commands and decrees I am giving you today, all these curses will come upon you and overtake you"* (Deuteronomy 28:15).

God gives us His law to protect us from behaviors that can harm us and steal our calling. God forbids sex outside of marriage, for example, not to limit our joy but to ensure it. Fidelity not only protects a person from incurable sexually transmitted diseases, but studies show it is also a requirement for emotional intimacy. The reality is: What God says, God means for our good.

Parents who say no and mean no help a child to understand the finality of God's Word and law and put in place the concept of lordship. A well-disciplined child recognizes that someone who is more powerful, wiser, and in a position of authority over him has the right to require submission and obedience. His parents taught him that obedience is a reasonable request. As the child matures, he is therefore inclined to yield his will to the Lord Jesus.

Finally, when yes means yes and no means no, parents teach their child that God's Word is reliable. Because they meant what they said, the child believes that God meant what He said. What God said will happen! The child grows up believing that God will keep His Word and faithfully perform it.

So is my word that goes out from my mouth: It will not return to me empty, but will accomplish what I desire and achieve the purpose for which I sent it. (Isaiah 55:11)

How do we help our children to develop a healthy response to authority—especially God's authority? Our disciplinary model is critical. If we are rigid and dictatorial, our children are likely to grow up fearing and resisting authority. If we are soft and lenient, our children may disregard and scorn authority when they are older. Demanding cooperation while showing empathy for our children, however, establishes in them a healthy pattern of contrition that carries over to adulthood.

Dictators engender fear. Nursemaids tend to coddle. Coaches inspire trust and devotion. To encourage a healthy response to authority, you need to shun the roles of the dictator and nursemaid and become a coach. Good coaches insist on complete cooperation but do not shame or humiliate their players. When your child refuses to clean up his room, calmly command, "I know you're frustrated; nevertheless, you will clean up your room." When your daughter stayed up late the night before, remind her, "Tonight you must go to bed early. I'm sorry; I know you feel bad about that." Acknowledging your child's feelings while remaining firm assures her that it is safe to comply—that your authority has her best interests in mind.

When authority is exercised in a loving way, a child is no longer obligated to engage in anxious efforts to control an environment that may be beyond his ability to negotiate. A child can easily feel overwhelmed if he believes he must take care of himself—too much freedom is nerve-wracking. (Life is hard enough for an adult to manage!) When a parent steps in and takes charge, a child is free to rest in his parent's care and protection. He may even experience relief as he lowers his sword and permits his parents to provide structure and guidance through discipline. Encounters with parental authority like these effect a positive response to authority—especially to God's.

Dictators engender fear, and nursemaids tend to coddle, but coaches inspire trust and devotion.

If authority is exercised in hurtful ways, however—either harshly or negligently—letting go of control and yielding to rightful authority is no longer considered a safe option. Fearing those in power, the child is left to fend for himself and strives to gain more control in order to protect himself.

Typically, he becomes willful and defiant. Ironically, the more control he seeks, the more out of control he becomes.

After a stressful day at work, Sam's parents frequently came home too tired and preoccupied with their own needs to discipline him properly. Sam often felt like he could get away with anything and his parents wouldn't care. Their indifferent attitude toward his behavior made him anxious and insecure. He felt unsafe and unloved. In an effort to gain a sense of security, he began to bully those around him. Dominating and intimidating others was Sam's way of asserting control over his environment and feeling safe. Today, as a Christian adult, Sam's marriage is in trouble. His wife reports that he is verbally abusive and overbearing. Apparently, Sam carried over into his marriage many of the unhealthy patterns of self-protection he developed as a child.

Sam wants to save his marriage and agrees that he is domineering at times. Yet he reports that if he doesn't protect himself in the relationship, no one else will. He also shares that trust has never been easy for him and that "letting go of control feels like I'm gonna die." Sam's compelling need to be in control can be traced to the lack of discipline and focused attention he received as a child.

His intense need to protect himself affects his relationship with God as well. He struggles with letting go of patterns of self-protection and trusting God to take care of him. He reasons on an emotional level that since his parents were unable to take charge of his life and provide structure and security, it is unlikely that God will. In Sam's mind, surrendering his efforts to defend himself renders him vulnerable and helpless—it seems self-destructive.

A child who admits he is wrong and surrenders his position must be sure that he will not be run through with his own sword.

In order to respond to God's lordship in humility and obedience, children need to know that it is safe to submit their wills to reasonable authority. They need parents who will treat them with respect and dignity when they humble themselves—parents who will not take advantage of them when they are contrite and vulnerable. For instance, a child who admits he is wrong and surrenders his position must be sure that he will not be run through with his own sword. Rather than a response like, "Well, you should be sorry!" parents should graciously accept their child's heartfelt confession and reassure him of their love. "Yes, I forgive you. Come give me a hug." A child also needs his parents to be reasonable and to allow him an opportunity to make a respectful appeal about what may seem like unfair consequences or unrealistic expectations.

Kids who are raised in homes where it is not safe to say "Sorry" often grow up with a tendency to avoid responsibility for their faults and sin. As adults, when wrongdoing is blatant, they may half-heartedly apologize, "If I hurt you, I'm sorry," or they may rationalize, "I shouldn't have said what I did, but you made me so angry!" in order to avoid what they assume will be more blame and humiliation. In addition, children whose trust has been broken tend to be suspicious of authority and frequently find themselves at odds with employers and church leaders.

❧❧❧❧

Things were going fine for Rick at church until the pastor didn't go for his idea to expand the Sunday school program. As soon as Rick received word that the pastor had a different plan, he felt hurt and angry. "Once again," he thought to himself, "I'm dealing with a dictatorship." Gathering up his family, he began another search for a new church home. "We've gotta go where the leadership isn't so heavy handed," he shared with his friends and family.

Rick was raised in a home where authority was unreasonable and unsafe. His father was an alcoholic who verbally abused him. His mother was manipulative and controlled his behavior by withdrawing her love and humiliating him with sarcastic remarks. Throughout his childhood, Rick never felt safe yielding to authority—submission meant the threat of annihilation. These feelings carried over into his adult life where, today, Rick is quick to judge those in any form of leadership as oppressive and abusive, and he is slow to appreciate the protection and peace that leadership can provide.

Our kids need to know that it's safe to own their faults—that they will not be cruelly punished or humiliated for confessing their sin. Reassuring them of our love when they confess their failings, acknowledging their feelings as we discipline, and forgiving them completely when they admit their guilt enables our children to take responsibility for their sins and repent.

See Appendix G, "Discipline Checklist," for help in disciplining your children in a way that enables them to develop a healthy response to authority.

How to Enforce Limits

One of the first things we can do to meet our children's needs for limits is to clearly communicate them. Many times children fail to meet our expectations because they don't know what they are. A posted list of "house rules" may be helpful.

When our children were in their early elementary years, we gathered everyone together and sat around the dinner table for a family meeting. I asked each member to state the most important rules of our house. We came up with ten and formed a family covenant. I was amazed at how enthusiastic the kids were about this project. I think they appreciated our trust in them—they were harder on themselves than we would have been. I also believe that creating a list of rules that Mom and Dad would be accountable for keeping was especially appealing to them. Below is the unedited version of our first family covenant. Before we placed it on the refrigerator, Mom and Dad did some amending.

Family Covenant

1. We will obey Jesus, who is our Lord.
2. We will not say bad words like "Shut up."
3. We will put things back where we found them.
4. We will be nice to kids we don't like. (Later revised to: "We will be kind to everyone.")
5. We will help each other.
6. We will do our chores without whining and complaining.
7. We will obey Mom and Dad, and Mom and Dad will obey God.

8. We will be cheerful and smile when we are disciplined. (Later revised to: "We will try to have a good attitude when we are disciplined." This seemed more realistic.)

9. When we hurt each other's feelings, we ask for forgiveness.

10. We will be kind and respectful to each other.

See Appendix H, "Rules of Our House: Writing a Family Covenant."

Once our children know our expectations, they need to know we intend to enforce them. As the saying goes, actions speak louder than words. Here is a general list of consequences:

1. Time out (one minute per year of age)

2. Denial of privileges like TV shows, special events, phone use, and time with friends

3. Early bedtimes

4. Removal of a toy or game

In my all-time favorite *Calvin and Hobbes* cartoon, Calvin is peeking his head in the front door and hollering to his mom. His mother sternly replies, "Calvin, stop yelling across the house! If you want to talk to me, walk over to the living room where I am!" Calvin hesitates, then casually strolls across the living room floor. Staring up innocently at his mom, he says, "I stepped in dog-doo. Where's the hose?"

Calvin's mom found out the hard way that compliance is not the same as character. Telling our children what to do is not enough if we want our children to think for themselves and to make their own moral decisions someday. Ultimately, we want them to please God for their own reasons, not ours. Our goal is self-control.

We develop self-control in our children by giving away control. The more choices we give away, the more opportunities our children have to grow in responsibility. Rather than giving your child an ultimatum, "Come to dinner now or else you don't get dessert," invite his cooperation. Give him a clear choice: "Do you want to come now to dinner and have dessert, or do you want to wait and miss dessert? You choose." Both are logical consequences, but the latter is phrased in such a way that it stimulates moral reasoning and promotes the development of self-control. "You choose" emphasizes the child's responsibility, not yours. The first consequence, "...or else you don't get dessert," makes the parent responsible for the child's choice. The parent becomes the disciplinarian, taskmaster, and "the-reason-why-I-can't-get-my-way." Our goal is to get out of the way so the child sees that he is responsible for his choice; he determines the outcome, apart from our involvement.

Let's look at another example: "Be home before eleven or you're grounded." Here again the parent is put in the role of dictator, which does little to help the teen see her responsibility to be home at a rea-

Ultimately, we want our children to please God for their own reasons, not ours. Our goal is self-control.

sonable hour. A better logical consequence would be, "It's your choice. You can be home at eleven and see your friends this weekend, or you can come home later and miss them." Both are logical consequences, but the latter statement places the burden of responsibility squarely on the teen, who now is able to see how her choice determines the activities of the weekend.

Giving your child choices does not mean you give up your authority. Make no mistake; as long as your child lives in your house, he is to be safely in your charge. You determine the choices. You enforce the limits. And you never give him more freedom than he can handle responsibly.

Children need moms and dads who are in charge. They feel safe when caring parents exercise their authority and hold them accountable for their actions. They feel at peace when someone wiser and more powerful brings order to a world they perceive as chaotic and frightening. Children who are well disciplined grow up with the understanding that God will also hold them accountable for their actions and that He expects them to follow the laws of His house as well. Well-disciplined kids are also better prepared to submit to God. Acquiescence to their parents' will was a safe experience—they were not humiliated or disgraced. Therefore, they anticipate the same kindness and respect from their Father in heaven when He requires obedience.

See Appendix I, "Family Communication Agreement," for establishing clear expectations and ground rules for communicating and resolving conflicts.

ACTION QUESTIONS

1. On the line below, put a mark indicating where you think you are in relation to your discipline style: Are you more of a dictator, coach, or nursemaid?

Dictator   **Coach**   **Nursemaid**

2. Do you listen to your child's feelings when you discipline him/her?

3. Do you allow your child to make a courteous appeal before you give him/her a consequence?

4. Do you shout, criticize, or shame your child when you discipline?

5. Do you avoid confronting your child and let things go? Do you think you are too passive?

6. Are your limits consistently enforced?

7. Do you give your child choices when you enforce limits? What are some ways you can rephrase your requests so that your child feels more responsible for his/her choices?

8. Does your child know what you expect from him/her? Do you have a list of your expectations—house rules—posted?

9. Do you forgive your child when he/she confesses his/her wrongdoing? Do you reassure him/her after discipline with a kind word or a hug?

10. Do you pray with your child and help him/her to seek God's forgiveness after he/she has been disciplined?

11. How is your tone of voice when you must discipline your child? Does it cause your child to feel frightened?

12. Are you satisfied with the way you manage your anger when you discipline? What steps can you take to handle it more effectively?

CHAPTER 10

Nearness:
The Fifth Emotional Need

There is probably no more powerful way to assure a child that he is loved and safe than to hold him in your arms. Your touch provides protection, comfort, warmth, and nourishment to his soul.

In the absence of touch, children show slower physiological and psychological development, especially among infants. Children need affection so badly that they can literally starve without it. A study conducted by psychologist Tiffany Field and published in *U.S. News & World Report* confirms,

> Premature infants who were massaged for 15 minutes three times a day gained weight 47 percent faster than preemies given standard intensive care nursery treatment: as little touching as possible. The preemies who were massaged weren't eating more; they just processed food more efficiently....Massaged preemies were more alert and aware of their surroundings when awake, while their sleep was deeper and more restorative. Eight months later, the massaged infants scored better on mental and motor tests.[1]

A lack of affection can cause children to hunger emotionally as well. Studies show that promiscuous men and women, especially teen girls, often report that their sexual encounters are a means of satisfying a longing to be touched and held. Dr. Marc Hollender, a noted psychiatrist, conducted a study of women who had had three or more unwanted pregnancies. The majority of these women shared that they were "consciously aware that sexual activity was a price to be paid for being cuddled and held."[2]

When parents demonstrate affection to their children, they assure them that they will not be deserted or left unprotected. Children think concretely—they are hands-on learners. Physical affection powerfully communicates to a child that he is safe and secure. As he feels the warmth of his parents' arms around him, he is convinced that he will not be abandoned. The parents' nearness also meets the children's need to know that they are worth holding on to. Affection communicates, "You are so dear to me, I want to hold you and keep you safe."

Hugging, holding, and cuddling your children deposit within them memories of comfort and security that are carried throughout their lives.

Hugging, holding, and cuddling a child deposit within his memory sensations of comfort and security that are carried throughout his life. Corrie ten Boom shares in her book *In My Father's House,*

> My security was assured in many ways as a child. Every night I would go to the door of my room in my nightie and call out, "Papa, I'm ready for bed." He would come to my room and pray with me before I went to sleep. I can remember that he always took time with us, and he would tuck the blankets around my shoulders very carefully, with his own characteristic precision. Then he would put his hand gently on my face and say, "Sleep well, Corrie...I love you."...Many years later in a concentration camp in Germany, I sometimes remembered the feeling of my father's hand on my face.[3]

The child who has felt the reassuring touch of her parents understands what it means to be comforted. She knows the sensation of melting into the protective arms of a parent. Her memories of physical affection provide, in part, a context for receiving solace from the presence of God. Because she received comfort from the nearness of her parents, she can perceive comfort from the nearness of God. As the child matures, the following verses render vital assurance to her:

So do not fear, for I am with you; do not be dismayed, for I am your God. I will strengthen you and help you; I will uphold you with my righteous right hand. (Isaiah 41:10)

For believers who grew up in homes where physical affection was genuine and abundant, the presence of God is more likely to be a vital experience than an abstract concept. The warmth of their parents' presence and the soothing sense of their touch fill the recesses of their memories. This information offers them a framework for appreciating the reality of God's presence.

And I will ask the Father, and he will give you another Counselor to be with you forever—the Spirit of truth. The world cannot accept him, because it neither sees him nor knows him. But you know him, for he lives with you and will be in you.
(John 14:16–17)

Parents who demonstrate physical affection provide children with an understanding of the nearness of God. God is seen as close, available, approachable, and protective. Such parents model a God who will never leave or forsake them. Children are inspired to seek a God like this and to pursue His calling upon their lives. They draw courage and hope from the promise of His continual presence.

Be strong and courageous. Do not be afraid or terrified because of them, for the LORD your God goes with you; he will never leave you nor forsake you. (Deuteronomy 31:6)

The following points offer practical suggestions for meeting your children's need for nearness:

1. Make it a point to hug your spouse and children every morning.

2. Keep in mind that your idea of desirable physical affection may be different than your child's.

3. Have an open arm policy with your children. Whenever they come near, open your arms.

4. When they want to wrestle, and you fear that if the match begins it may not stop (a very real concern), set a timer (kitchen timers are excellent) for five minutes and let them know that when the buzzer goes off, the bout is over. Move furniture out of the way and take care not to let the little ones wind up on the bottom of the pile.

5. If you're too tired to wrestle, find an alternative, like thumb wrestling, or "rock, scissors, paper."

6. Play horsey and give rides.

7. Sit down on the couch with your children, put your arms around them, and just hold them gently when they are feeling discouraged. No great words of wisdom are needed.

8. Drawing your children to your side while reading the Bible is a way to touch them physically and spiritually as well.

9. Brush your teenage daughter's hair while watching a video.

10. Gently shove, twist, tweak, tousle, punch, and poke your teenage son.

11. Put your arm around your daughter or hold her hand while walking in public.

12. Sit close together while reading a book or watching a video.

13. Give rides on your back up to bed.

14. Kiss and hug your children before bed each night.

ACTION QUESTIONS

1. Do you have an open-arms policy with your child? When he/she is near, do you open your arms?

2. Does your child seem resistant to your demonstrations of affection? Find out why. Perhaps you are too affectionate, or maybe you are too rough. Perhaps there is hidden resentment and mistrust.

3. Do you make a special effort to hold each of your children every day?

Chapter Notes

1. Shannon Brownlee and Traci Watson, "The Senses," *U.S. News & World Report*, January 13, 1997, 55.
2. Dr. Marc Hollender, "The Wish to Be Held," *Archives of General Psychiatry* 22 (1970): 445–453.
3. Corrie ten Boom, *In My Father's House* (Boston, Mass.: G. K. Hall & Co., 1976), 78–79.

CHAPTER 11

Time:
The Sixth Emotional Need

A rmand Nicholi, a Harvard University psychiatrist, said this in regard to a child's needs for a parent's time:

> Time is like oxygen. There is a minimal amount that is needed to survive. Less than that amount may cause permanent damage.[1]

The child who does not feel like he is the center of her parents' attention and their main priority in life will struggle over time with feelings of abandonment and rejection. As he matures, he will enter relationships cautiously, fearing rejection and more abandonment; or he may rush into relationships like a person on the brink of starvation, demanding and consuming every ounce of love his partner can muster.

Damage from a lack of parental involvement spills over into a child's relationship with God as well. He is likely to question, on an emotional level, God's promise to be with him at all times, especially during stressful circumstances, and resort to his own resources instead of God's. He reasons that if his parents didn't spend adequate time with him, why should God?

Mike is distant and aloof with his family. Though he is a good provider, he is quiet and withdrawn and seems unable to communicate, or uninterested in communicating, his feelings to his wife and children. He keeps God at arm's length as well. Though he attends church and prays, he handles life's difficulties in his own strength and is reluctant to fully depend on God for help.

Mike's parents were missionaries. He shares,

> My parents put me in a mission's boarding school when I was a child. I felt like an orphan most of the time. I was abused physically and sexually at the school while my parents were serving the Lord.

Mike shut down emotionally to endure the pain of his parents' neglect. As he was growing up, he determined that it was too painful to depend on others (including God) and decided to handle things on his own.

When we reflect a God who is near, gracious, and caring, our children are able to trust God to stick with them during the hard times.

Mike's parents modeled a God who was neglectful and unavailable. Parents who spend time with their children, in contrast, reflect a God who is at hand, gracious, and caring. Children from homes like these are able to trust God to stick with them during the hard times and to help them overcome obstacles. They know God will not forsake them because their parents didn't. They gain strength from verses that promise, *"And surely I am with you always, to the very end of the age"* (Matthew 28:20).

More than our time, children need our involvement. Just being in the same room with our children—chopping carrots in the kitchen, reading a newspaper in the living room, or watching TV—does not always register as love. Our children are looking for an emotional connection with us. They need our attention as well as our attendance.

Tom grew up with parents who were present but "not there." Though they were home almost every night, they were too intoxicated to give him the love he needed. As an adult, Tom struggles with a prevailing sense of loneliness and has a great deal of difficulty trusting others.

Theresa's mom was home every night as well. The financial pressures of being a single parent, however, preoccupied her attention and drained her emotionally. Theresa grew up feeling alone and unloved by God and others.

Children need time—both quality and quantity time. Good relationships require focused attention (quality) and lots of it (quantity). Kids need parents who spend special times centered on their children's interests and concerns, and they need parents who are available.

The Washington Post reported a study of more than 270,000 children in 600 communities in which children who spent at least four evenings a week at home with their families and had regular, in-depth conversations with their parents did better in three categories. They performed better in school, were less likely to use alcohol or drugs, and were less apt to be sexually active.[2]

Children feel the full measure of our love when we play with them. We enter into the moment and give ourselves away as we wrestle, chase, laugh, and lovingly tease. Parents who play communicate, "You're the center of my attention. You're important to me. You have me all to yourself."

Children benefit spiritually as well when parents spend time playing with them. More than any other demonstration of love, having fun with our kids teaches them that God is not just present with us; He is interested in us. When we enjoy our children, we model a God who delights in His children.

The LORD your God is with you, he is mighty to save. He will take great delight in you, he will quiet you with his love, he will rejoice over you with singing. (Zephaniah 3:17)

Most of us would be glad to spend more time with our kids. The question is, how?

An honest look at our date books may reveal that the problem isn't so much a shortage of time, but how we spend it. Though many work the hours they do to simply put food on the table (single parents, for instance), it seems that the majority of us work to put stuff in the garage. Though it may feel, at times, like we are compelled against our will to carry a staggering workload, the truth is that we have choices. We chose the job; we agreed to the overtime; we chose to stay.

"Daddy, I don't want to talk to you on the phone anymore; I want you to come home." With that, the six-year-old boy handed the phone to his mother. Bill (the father) was weeping on the other end of the line. Suddenly, his six-digit salary seemed small. "I'm coming home," he said. And he did. He quit his demanding job and took a $70,000 cut in pay to work as a schoolteacher. "Things are tight," his wife said, "but we are a family now, and it's worth it."

Bill decided that his kids needed his time more than his sizable income. More and more parents are opting to economize everything from food to entertainment to household items in order to reduce consumption and increase family time.

Sarah was an IBM executive; her husband was a pastor. When the children were born, she decided to stay home to ensure that their emotional needs were met and that Christlikeness was formed in their character. Financially, things were a strain, but they lived simply and made things work. When her children entered their late elementary years, Sarah went to night school to study law. Today, she practices elderly law (wills, probate, and Medicare law) out of her home and keeps her appointments during school hours so she can give her children the time they need when they arrive home.

Like Bill, Sarah changed her lifestyle to accommodate her children's need for a mother's time. For many hardworking parents (especially single parents), however, the frantic pace and extra work has less to do with materialism and greed than with making the mortgage payments and putting food on the table. Most people simply can't afford to walk away from their jobs. Still, even in the direst of circumstances, there are ways to manage our schedules that maximize time with the family.

Work hours. Some parents may be able to rearrange their work schedules in order to have more time with the kids. Look for flexibility in a new job or negotiate for better hours with your current one. Go to work later so you can have breakfast with your kids and drive them to school. Or go to work earlier so you can be home when the bus drops them off in the afternoon.

Dinnertime. Having dinner as a family ensures a regular time for sharing and interaction. Studies show that having dinner together is a major determinant of happy and secure families. Focus on pleasurable and fun topics by asking questions like, "What was the best thing that happened to you today?"

Vacation. You can't afford not to. Even a short, get-away weekend provides an opportunity to get to know one another better. A single mom who works as a hairdresser rents a campsite at the same beach every year. Her children have been tenting the same week in July since they were old enough to walk. This mom says it's economical and a great way for her busy family to build memories and closeness.

Television. Turn it off and reconnect with the kids. According to a survey conducted by Mike Yorkey, among "successful" dads, 29 percent don't watch any TV during the week and 61 percent view no more than two hours a night.[3]

Find a common recreational interest. Bike riding, hiking, or swimming can bring families together and offer health benefits as well.

Date nights. Schedule a date night once a month with each of your children. Start when they are young so that a pattern of honest and open communication is established before sensitive issues like love, sex, and dating begin to surface.

With careful planning, resourcefulness, and commitment, even the busiest parents can make time for their children.

ACTION QUESTIONS

1. Do you have at least one meal together as a family each day?

2. Do you have a hobby you can share with your child?

3. When was the last time you got alone with your child and had a one-on-one conversation?

4. Do you take time to do something fun with your child (apart from TV) even for a short amount of time each day?

5. Do you read to your child at night?

6. What about scheduling a date night with each child on your family calendar?

7. Do you have an inexpensive get-away planned for this year?

8. Do you need to make some changes in your work schedule?

9. If you turned off the TV this evening, what could you do to have fun with your family?

Chapter Notes

1. As quoted in "Respect: Developing Kids Who Do," North Heartland Community Church, May 14, 1995. <http://northheartland.org/1995/051495m.htm> (February 13, 2006)

2. Jacqueline Salmon, "Finding the Time to Be a Family," *Washington Post Weekly*, May 12, 1997.

3. Mike Yorkey, "Time Well Spent," *New Man*, June 1996, 54–56.

CHAPTER 12

Support:
The Seventh Emotional Need

What is it about young children and stone walls? It seems there is this unwritten rule among children: Things that are hard and sharp and high enough from which to fall and break an arm must be climbed. This indisputable law of childhood has a way of turning our peaceful family outings into untold parental angst. My first reaction is always, "Get down from there; you'll fall!" But then a little hand reaches out and beckons me to support him in his daring venture. At that moment, a tension rises within me: "Do I let him go or hold him back?" Raw parental instinct says, "Hold him back. Don't let him go," but wisdom says, "If you don't let him go, he may never learn to climb."

If our children are to ascend to their callings, they will need the freedom to fall—but not too far. They will need guidance, protection, and encouragement to safely step out into their callings. Like toddlers learning to walk, they need us to hold their hands as we let them go. This need for support is especially acute when our children enter their late teens.

Adolescence is typically a time of conflicting emotion for children. Older children are excited about gaining new independence but anxious about increased responsibility. Specifically, they worry about not having the necessary knowledge and decision-making abilities to manage their freedom wisely.

Most parents assume that older children so relish their freedom that parental support is unwanted. This is not true. Though autonomy is important to teens, they still want counsel, and even behavioral boundaries, according to a study conducted by the University of Tel Aviv. The study of children aged eight to eighteen showed that younger children wanted time together with their parents and lots of treats, whereas teens wanted guidance and lots of freedom. Even the seventeen- and eighteen-year-olds still wanted both autonomy and support.[1]

Mary, age twenty-three, is glad for her independence, but after two years of student loans and credit card debt, together with a new car and apartment, she admits that she's in over her head and wishes her parents had been more involved in her decisions. "It was a little more than I could handle," she confesses.

Regular guidance and support have spiritual benefits as well. By gently holding our children's hands as they step out into an unknown future, we model God's protective care and fatherly guidance:

> *It was I who taught Ephraim to walk, taking them by the arms;*
> *but they did not realize it was I who healed them. I led them*
> *with cords of human kindness, with ties of love; I lifted the yoke*
> *from their neck and bent down to feed them.* (Hosea 11:3–4)

See Appendix J, "Raising Fear-less Kids in a Fearful World," for more on how your support and encouragement can inspire your child to turn from fear to faith.

Marty, a forty-year-old pastor, shares how childhood memories of his mother's enthusiastic support help him better understand God today:

I can still see my mother on the edge of the wrestling mat waving her arms and pounding the red canvas. I was probably fifteen at the time and wrestling varsity. Though I'm sure she wished I had taken up tennis, she eagerly supported me and never missed a match. Once she got so excited during a bout, the ref had to ask her to return to the bleachers and sit down. Sometimes I see God like this. He is on the edge of the mat rooting me on like my Mom. Only in this match, I'm not wrestling against flesh and blood but against spiritual forces that seek to destroy my life and those I love. God is also like my mother, in that, if my opponent were to overwhelm me and threaten me with bodily harm, He would storm the mat and throw my opponent into the bleachers.

We model an image of God that is true to the Bible when we provide support that does not smother or overprotect. We reflect God's desire for our children to "go for it" and to live radically for Him. *"Take nothing for the journey except a staff—no bread, no bag, no money in your belts,"* Jesus said to His disciples (Mark 6:8). God may call us to leave our methods of provision and completely depend on Him as we seek to fulfill His calling. As we do, He promises to fully support us, to be there for us, and to cheer us on.

> *For I am the LORD, your God, who takes hold of your right hand and says to you, Do not fear; I will help you.* (Isaiah 41:13)

If kids need our support, why are they so often reluctant to take it? We offer advice and our daughters tune us out. We try to console, and our teens deny they are hurt. What do we do?

Children, especially teens, are very protective of their growing need for independence. They worry that acknowledging their need for support will provide anxious parents an occasion to regain control of their lives and to make decisions without their consent. From a teen's point of view, nothing must be allowed to hinder his all-important climb toward independence. Though this passion for freedom and self-determination must be tempered, it should be regarded as normal and, in fact, God-given. Indeed, it is a child's motivation for growing up and assuming adult responsibility.

Teens feel put down when parents step in and take over their problems without permission. The college-bound teen, for instance, is likely to feel disrespected by her parents when they tell her, "Quit your summer camp counseling and make some real money." The young man who fails to finish painting his neighbor's house on time is devastated when his parents apologize for him and agree to refund the money. It's no wonder that our youth are reluctant to ask for our help if we take away their chance to be involved in decisions that affect their lives.

> By gently holding our children's hands as they step out into an unknown future, we model God's protective care and fatherly guidance.

Children and teens are far less resistant to our support when we affirm their autonomy and problem-solve with them. Rather than pulling rank and telling them what to do, we can coach our children to think for themselves. Instead of commanding, "Just bear down and get your homework done!" or coldly lecturing, "It took me many years to learn to work first, play later," we can support our children by getting them to analyze their behavior and its consequences. We can say, for instance, "What will happen if you don't get your assignment in tomorrow?" We can then help them to choose alternatives and solutions by asking, "What subject will you do first? What time do you plan on going to bed? If you wait until after dinner, will there be any time for fun later?"

Jesus understood the secret of giving advice: He never told anyone anything He could ask. In the following verses, note how He used questions to help men and women think for themselves: *"Who do people say the Son of Man is?"* (Matthew 16:13). *"Judas, are you betraying the Son of Man with a kiss?"* (Luke 22:48). *"John's baptism—where did it come from? Was it from heaven, or from men?"* (Matthew 21:25).

As strange as it may seem, supporting our children may mean allowing them to suffer the consequences of their decisions. To deny them the fruit of their choices—bad fruit included—is to deny them true ownership of the decision-making process. Though our parenting instincts yearn to shield our children from painful consequences, intervening prematurely usually does more damage than good. It usurps our children's independence and undermines their confidence. In addition, overprotecting our kids robs them of an outstanding education. Failure is an excellent teacher. Tina, a forty-year-old mom, shared, "It hurt

> *We model an image of God that is true to the Bible when we provide support that does not smother or overprotect.*

when my mother refused to bring my clarinet to a high school recital (I left it on the dining room table again), but I knew she did it for my good. She loved me enough to teach me to be responsible. I borrowed the band director's and never forgot to bring my own again." Unless your children's choices put them at risk of serious physical, emotional, or spiritual injury, do not rush to bail them out of poor decisions.

In short, healthy support means giving our kids choices—lots of choices. It should be our motto that we do not do anything for our children that they can do for themselves. Beginning in the preschool years, we should ask, "You choose: Do you want to wear the white pants or the red pants to church?" Later, in high school, the choices become more significant: "As far as this trip with your friends, I'm leaving the choice up to you. I only ask that you pray about it." The more choices we allow our children, the more confidence we demonstrate in them and the more trust we build. By giving them lots of practice in making choices, we also help them to grow in decision-making skills. To help you with this, I've included Appendix K, "Decision-Making Matrix." Use this chart to work through possible choices and their outcomes with your child.

Giving our children choices does not mean we give up parental control and protection, however. Make no mistake; our children are to be safely in our charge throughout their childhoods—even in their teen years. As a general rule, permit a child only as much freedom as the child can handle responsibly. No more, no less. Giving your child more freedom than he can handle responsibly places him in danger. A daughter, for instance, who has shown a tendency to compromise her values to gain peer approval perhaps should not be given the choice to go to the mall with her friends, unless you go with her. To do otherwise may set her up for more temptation than she can resist.

If our children are to ascend to their callings, they need the freedom to fall and the assurance of our support.

When parents coach rather than command, they earn their children's trust. By asking rather than telling children what to do, parents demonstrate respect for their children's personhood and all-important goal of independence. Children who are convinced that their parents have their best interests in mind are willing to acknowledge their need for support.

Children who freely receive their parents' support are capable of freely receiving God's guidance and help. They know that, just as their mother and father honored their individuality and respected their right to determine their destinies, God will as well. As adults, they freely seek God for help without fear of being shamed, dominated, or abandoned.

They are confident that God will not take advantage of their vulner-ability—He will not impatiently squash their ideas or angrily demand His way over theirs. In matters of their calling, He will graciously offer His assistance and enthusiastically cheer them on toward their goals. Our children will see Him as a *"refuge and strength, an ever-present help in trouble"* (Psalm 46:1) and One who *"will guide* [them] *into all truth"* (John 16:13).

In what specific ways do children need support? More than any material assistance, our children need our prayers. They will need the resources of heaven—God's encouragement, direction, and provision—to fulfill their divine callings. Children also need us to guide them into their ordained vocations. Using the DNA Analysis Survey, we can help them to identify their gifts and interests, offering them direction in regard to their callings. They need us to teach them about the Bible—how to read it and how to obey it. As they get older, they will also need our advice in decisions about finance, marriage, and educational training—with the condition that it is

> More than anything, our children need our prayers and the resources of heaven—God's encouragement, direction, and provision—to fulfill their divine callings.

offered with respect and unselfish motives. Finally, they will need clear boundaries about what they should expect and should not expect from us in terms of financial support and use of the car or home.

If our children are to ascend to their callings, they need the freedom to fall and the assurance of our support. They need us to challenge them in areas of giftedness; at the same time, they need us to protect them from overwhelming discouragement and disappointment. To set our children free without guidance and boundaries is to delay their destinies indefinitely, but to deny them the freedom to try and fail is to deny them their destinies entirely.

ACTION QUESTIONS

1. Do you attend your child's performances or games?

2. Do you help your older child to assess his/her situation and then come up with solutions to his/her problem, or do you simply tell him/her what to do?

3. Do you encourage your child to take risks? To try new interests? Do you challenge your child to excel in areas of giftedness by offering him/her better classes, training, or coaching?

4. Do you do things for your child that he/she can do for himself? Picking out clothes? Making the bed? Making lunch? Laundry? Ironing clothes?

5. How do you know when your child is in over his/her head and is in danger? Think about things he/she is involved in right now—friendships, schoolwork, jobs, hobbies, and forms of entertainment. How would you know if he/she needed your intervention?

6. Do you give your child as much freedom as he/she can handle responsibly? TV viewing? Friendships? Outings? Sports? Money? School activities? Shopping? Selection of musical artists? How would you know when your child is being irresponsible with these things? What would be the signs?

7. Do you pray daily for your child to fulfill his/her calling?

8. Do you train your child to know God's Word? Do you have a quiet time together? Do you read the Bible to your child?

9. Would you say you are in touch with where your child is emotionally right now? What dreams does he/she have for his/her life? What does your child wish for most? What is he/she worried about this week? Who is your child's favorite movie star, musician? Have there been any changes in his/her mood, sleep habits, or eating habits? Who are the primary social influences in his/her life right now?

10. Do you respect your child's privacy (unless you have a reasonable concern about your child's well-being)?

PARENTS NEEDS ASSESSMENT

When a child's seven emotional needs are met, a foundation is laid for unimpeded pursuit of God and His unique plan for his life. Recall that "PARENTS" needs refer to Protection, Acceptance, Recognition, Enforced Limits, Nearness, Time, and Support. How well are you meeting your children's emotional needs? The survey below may help you to determine this. Answer this assessment for each of your children.

(5) All the time (4) Mostly (3) Sometimes (2) Rarely (1) Never

_____1. Do you compliment your child when he/she excels in his/her area of gifting?

_____2. Do you affirm your child in activities in which he/she shows interest? Even those interests that you do not share?

_____3. Do you have at least one family meal a day where everyone is present?

_____4. Do you take off one day a week to spend with your family, apart from work or special projects?

_____5. Do you administer discipline respectfully?

_____6. Do you pray daily with your child?

_____7. Do you allow your child to take risks when physical and emotional danger is minimal?

_____8. Do you attend your child's special events?

_____9. Do you have a bedtime routine?

_____10. Do you hold, hug, kiss, and tussle your child on a daily basis?

_____**Subtotal**

(5) Never (4) Rarely (3) Sometimes (2) Mostly (1) All the time

_____1. Are you given to moods and irritability?

_____2. Do you strike (slap or spank) your child in anger?

_____3. Are you currently engaged in a life-controlling problem that reduces the amount of time and care you can give your children (addictions, depression, obsessions)?

_____4. Do you speak disrespectfully (sarcasm, name-calling, shouting) to your child?

_____5. Do you feel like your child frustrates your goals?

_____6. Do you expect your child to do as good a job as you would do?

_____7. Do you bring your problems home from work so that they preoccupy your attention?

_____8. Do marital problems negatively affect your mood and energy at home?

_____9. Do you tend to interrupt your child and make quick judgments?

_____10. Are you too busy to deal with your child's underlying problems?

_____Subtotal

_____Grand Total (combine subtotals)

Do you feel like a worthless "slimeball" after taking this survey? (If so, you have friends. See the Disclaimer for Guilty Parents below.)

If your _grand total_ was between 20 and 40, your children need you to develop some better methods of demonstrating love. They need your help in building a strong emotional foundation that will support their callings. If you scored between 41 and 60, your children have an emotional foundation that will, with the development of better parenting skills on your part, carry them through to their destinies. If you scored between 61 and 100, your children are well on their way to their callings.

Disclaimer for Guilty Parents

Most of us are painfully aware of our bad habits and moments of parental failure. There is usually no doubt in our minds that other moms and dads are doing a far better job. Although a healthy dose of guilt can motivate us to change, excessive guilt can be debilitating.

For those of us who are weighed down by parent-guilt, let me offer this suggestion: Dispel the myth of the perfect family. There is nothing more demoralizing to moms and dads than the illusion of perfect marriages, perfect children, and perfect parents.

Fact #1: You and your family will never be perfect. You married a sinner, your spouse married a sinner, and together you made little sinners. But here's the good news: It's because you aren't perfect that Jesus left heaven in search of you! *"For the Son of man is come to seek and to save that which was lost"* (Luke 19:10 KJV). He came to save you because you needed Him. Confess your failure to God. Let Him forgive you and begin to turn your sad ending into a new beginning. Those who have failed most miserably are often the first to enjoy God's plan for success.

Fact #2: The family at church that looks like they have it all together doesn't. Go ahead and ask them (I do), and they will tell you that they need God as much as you. If they do have a measure of success, it is because they accept, rather than reject, their brokenness. Your family would be a lot healthier if you did away with the yoke of perfectionism. Admit your faults and needs up front. Rather than striving in your own strength, honestly confess your problems to others and God. William Shakespeare once said, "Striving to be better, oft we mar what's well."[2] More than any attempt to attain perfection, honest acceptance of our limitations provides the opportunity for real change and real communication.

Therefore confess your sins to each other and pray for each other so that you may be healed. (James 5:16)

Chapter Notes

1. "The Age of Ambivalence," *Psychology Today*, November/December 1992, 20.
2. Shakespeare, *King Lear*, 1.4.369.

Chapter 13

Taste and See
That the Lord Is Good

In the Irish movie comedy *Waking Ned Divine*, a young boy named Morris asks the village priest if he's ever seen "Him."

"Who?" the priest asks.

"Jesus," the boy queries.

"No, not really."

"Well, have you met Him?" asks the boy.

"In a way," the priest cautiously responds.

"How do you get paid?" the boy asks.

"My pay is spiritual," the priest replies. "Do you feel drawn to the church, Morris?" he adds, wondering if the boy's curiosity is an indication of a call to the priesthood.

"I don't think so," Morris replies. "I could never work for someone I've never met and that didn't pay."

Morris was right. How can you devote yourself to someone you've never met and who doesn't take care of your needs?

By consistently meeting our children's emotional needs, we help them develop healthy capacities to trust and an accurate understanding of God. One thing is still needed if our children are to seek after God, however. Our children must meet Him.

How do we introduce our children to Jesus? We must whet their appetites.

It all begins with hunger. Jesus said, *"Blessed are those who hunger and thirst for righteousness, for they will be filled"* (Matthew 5:6). No hunger, no filling; it's that simple. We can cook up a tremendous meal, but unless our kids are hungry, our efforts are in vain.

Have you ever tried to make your two-year-old eat his dinner when he isn't hungry? He will stick his food in every opening of his head but his mouth. You cannot make your child eat unless he is hungry. Similarly, you cannot make your child seek after God unless he is spiritually hungry. Fortunately, God, in His great mercy, has placed in the heart of man a yearning for His presence. Ecclesiastes 3:11 says, *"He has also set eternity in the hearts of men."*

> Jesus was a kid-magnet. The good news is that He still is.

Deep within the heart of man, there exists a primordial longing for God. The great theologian of antiquity, Augustine, spoke of this felt need when he wrote, "You made us for Yourself, and our hearts are restless until they rest in You."[1] Augustine would contend that all of us have a natural appetite for God that provokes us to seek after Him.

We see in the Gospels that children wanted to be near Jesus. They played at His feet, sat on His lap, ate lunch with Him as He fed the five thousand, attended His sermons, and welcomed Him with praise as He triumphantly entered Jerusalem riding on a colt. Jesus was a kid-magnet. He still is. By tapping into our children's natural interest in God, we can lead them into an encounter with Him.

There is another natural craving that is common to man, and in particular, children. Deep within the primordial desires of a human being, there exists an appetite for ice cream. Certainly, there is no debate about this among children.

Since we were so successful in introducing our children to the taste of ice cream, perhaps we may apply the same steps toward introducing our children to the taste of God? After all, the Bible says, *"Taste and see that the Lord is good"* (Psalm 34:8). God tastes sweet to the soul, just as ice cream tastes sweet to the mouth. *"How sweet are your words to my taste, sweeter than honey to my mouth!"* (Psalm 119:103).

How We Introduce Our Children to Ice Cream

1. Model Your Love

The best way to arouse interest in your children for ice cream is to demonstrate your love for it. Ice cream lovers are experts at modeling their love. You can see it on their faces, and you can hear it in their voices: "MMMMMMMMMM! Wow, try the mocha fudge!"

Beth, our youngest, was two when we officially introduced her to ice cream. True to two-year-old form, the first time we asked her if she wanted to taste our ice cream, her response was a resounding "No!" But after watching us devour the weird looking ball in a cone and listening to our slurps, she decided to try it. "Taaaaste? Taaaaste?" she whined. "Do you want to try some ice cream?" we asked again. "Nooo—kay," she shouted. One taste later, she was hooked for life.

Modeling a love for ice cream implies that we (a) like it ourselves, and (b) spend time with our child when we eat it. Modeling our love for God follows the same pattern. First, we need to love God ourselves. We can't give away what we don't have. By regularly attending church, eagerly obeying God, and delighting in worship and Bible study, we communicate the idea that knowing God is a joy. Second, we need to involve our children in our spiritual life. If they are to witness our enthusiasm, they need to be with us when we demonstrate it. Here are some practical ways to model your love for God:

- Worshipping to a praise tape with your child.

- Praying with your children enthusiastically.

- Praying with your children when they are sad, hurt, or afraid.

- Reading God's Word out loud and making it exciting for kids.

- Humbling yourself before others and saying, "I am sorry. I was wrong; please forgive me" and then praying for God to forgive you.

- Displaying love to family members by not being selfish with your time, money, and interests.

- Eagerly obeying God.

Ken Taylor, best known for his paraphrase of the Bible, *The Living Bible*, says this about how the model of his parents cultivated his hunger for God:

> I am also thankful that my parents had a family prayer time every morning after breakfast before we children rushed to the school bus. My brothers and I went into the day with our parents' blessings and prayers. The family prayer time included a Scripture reading and an explanation from Dad when the passage was hard to understand. Then each of us prayed about matters of personal concern and for one another....
>
> As I grew up, I saw Mother and Dad reading their Bibles frequently, and they encouraged us to get into the same habit. Dad, a United Presbyterian pastor, used to tell us: "You fellows will never amount to much for God unless you get into the Word and the Word gets into you."[2]

2. Offer Variety

Vanilla can get boring after a while. Kids want variety. Kids love flavors like Bubble Gum, Gummy Worm Mint, and Death by Chocolate with chocolate chips.

God offers many exciting ways to experience His goodness, as well. As parents, we can provide our children with a variety of thrilling mediums and methods for knowing God.

- Get them a good Bible. Children love owning their own Bibles—although they will lose them every Sunday at church. Take your children to the local Christian bookstore and have them pick out their own.

- Read to your children from a Bible version that is geared for their age range. When children are young, find a children's Bible with colorful pictures and easy-to-understand text. When they are older, read from a Bible that has age-appropriate discussion starters and Bible-knowledge questions.

- In reading from any Bible translation, skip over text your child does not understand. Don't get bogged down in the "begats"—concentrate on portions in which your child shows interest.

- Read inspirational books aloud—books that you especially like. Your enthusiasm will be contagious. Try C. S. Lewis's *The Chronicles of Narnia,* John Bunyan's *The Pilgrim's Progress,* or Hannah Hurnard's *Hinds' Feet on High Places.*

- Make everything around you a prop. A blanket can be the curtain of the Holy of Holies, a chair can be Mt. Carmel, and a box can be the wall of Jericho.

- Don't feel obligated to finish the whole story; let your children's interest be your guide. Quit while they are still interested. Try not to overdo it.

- Incorporate movement into the story. Role-play a Bible story. After reading the story, act it out. Example: Pretend to hold up Moses' hands, swing an imaginary sling, or play Miriam's tambourine.

- When reading, change your voice to fit the characters and humorously act out a scene.

- Use puppets, stuffed animals, army men, even Barbie and Ken to act out a story.

- Make Scripture memory fun through game formats. Ask your local Christian bookstore for a children's curriculum on Scripture memory.

- Have on hand a variety of kid's worship and praise tapes.

- Have on hand lots of age-appropriate Christian videos.

- Pray together. Don't force your children to pray; model simple prayers. Remember, little prayers for little people. Go around in a circle and encourage your children to tell Jesus one thing or to pray just one word. Then go first and model it. We call this kind of prayer "popcorn prayer."

- Serve God together as a family. Your entire family can serve as ushers, greeters, teachers, musicians, and groundskeepers at church. Take a family mission trip: Serve at a soup kitchen or visit a foreign missionary from your church.

3. Serve Only the Purest Ingredients

Certain influences and experiences can spoil our children's appetite for God. Avoid exposure to media, Internet use, video games, and peer influence that may jeopardize a child's emotional and spiritual health.

Monitor and Screen Media Influence

Time magazine, in the spring of 1999, voiced the following call to arms in the wake of the Columbine High School bloodbath:

If there is a war to be fought, the critical beachhead is in the home....We'd all prefer that the porn, the neo-Nazis, the violent misogynists, and all the other floating trash of a cacophonous culture not wash up into our living rooms. But because they do, we are at least able to know the enemy. We can devise strategies to steer our children away from what's worst...toward what is best, even as they grow up much, much too fast.[3]

I ask you, is this an article from *Time* magazine or a promotional advertisement from Focus on the Family? Violence in schools has reached such epidemic proportions that parents all over the country are starting to wake up to the fact that something is very wrong with the youth culture. Christian parents are on the alert more than ever before, and they are learning how to put sources of cultural influence (video games, Hollywood media, and negative peer influence) in check before they pollute their children's minds and spoil their appetites for God.

As a parent, your first line of defense against menacing media influence is to control the flow. Set firm limits on the quality and quantity of suggestive messages that pour into the ears, minds, and spirits of your children. One statistic showed that children sit "passively in front of a TV screen for 28.5 hours each week"![4]

Monitor Peer Influence

Did you know that...

- the vast majority of first-time exposure to sexually explicit materials and sexual encounters takes place in peer relationships?

- first encounters with drug abuse are usually with peers?

- juvenile criminal offenses are conducted, in the majority of instances, in the company of peers?

- more than 7.5 million young people aged 12–17 reported using an illicit drug at least once, according to a 2003 study? And that "9.9 percent of student respondents nationwide tried marijuana for the first time before the age of 13, 28.7 percent had been offered, sold, or given an illegal drug on school property during the year preceding the survey, and 5.8 percent had used marijuana on school property one or more times during the 30 days preceding the survey"?[5]

By being proactive, you can help your child to avoid the pitfalls of negative peer influence. First, fill your child's social calendar with enough positive peer experiences that there is no room for negative ones! Discover who the positive influences are in your child's life and arrange times for them to get together.

Resorting to shame and intimidation in order to motivate our children to seek God only builds resentment and undermines trust.

Next, make your home a teen haven so that your child will invite her friends over. Always have lots of snacks on hand. "Scotchguard" the carpet. Try to relax. It's better to have them spill on your carpet than on a bar floor. Buy video games. Build a recreation room, if you can. Finish the unfinished basement. Keep your old furniture. Be willing to sacrifice. Buy a used foosball or ping-pong table. Invite other families with teens over to watch the Olympics or the Super Bowl.

Most importantly, stay abreast of your teen's social life. Insist on knowing whom your child is with and the reason your child is going out. Get involved at school, in after-school activities, and at church. Help out. Be available but avoid being intrusive, if possible. You don't need to unnecessarily embarrass your teens—that will happen naturally.

4. Do Not Force-Feed

No matter how sincere you are, hollering, "EAT YOUR ICE CREAM!" will not inspire interest. Your child is naturally drawn to what tastes good. You can relax and let the ice cream do the work.

Trusting God to woo our children is extremely difficult for most of us. Letting go of control when something so precious as our child's salvation is at stake grates against our deepest parental instinct—especially when we see how the world wants to devour them alive. Some of us are so fearful that we resort to shame and intimidation to motivate our children to seek God. Such methods only build resentment and undermine trust.

❧❧❧

My teenage daughter has been having a hard time adjusting to school this year, and I've been concerned that she isn't handling her difficulty with God's help. So this morning, when she woke up feeling grumpy and a little depressed, I went right to work on her. My first words were a frosty, "Listen, are you praying about this?" Was I compassionate and understanding? Did I hug her and listen to her feelings? No. Did I try to shame her and intimidate her into seeking God? Yes. I was so concerned for her well-being, I tried to force-feed her Jesus! I said, in effect, "Take your Jesus-medicine and feel better now!" If we are not careful, fear will cause us to intimidate our children into serving God.

There is nothing we can do to make our children seek God. We can predispose our children to trust in Him by providing a parent model that reflects God's love, but the rest is something that is outside our control. Children, like all human beings, do things for their reasons, not ours. They are motivated by their own personal needs, not by what we think is right or good.

The bottom line is this: We cannot motivate anyone to want anything. By exerting various types of pressure, we may be able to make our children conform to Christian standards—we may get them to act like Christians—but we can never make them want God. In fact, it's likely that our efforts to control their choices will spoil their genuine appetite for God.

5. Pray

You may not be able to make your child want to eat his dinner, but if you wait until he is hungry, he will want it for himself. Similarly, though you cannot make your child love God, you can wait until he has a need for Him, and then introduce him to Jesus.

Children, like all of us, are motivated by felt needs. Felt needs are those needs we are aware of and go out of our way to satisfy—physical hunger is an example.

What can we do to stimulate spiritual hunger? Pray. Pray for God to arouse a spiritual need in your child. Jesus said, *"No one can come to me unless the Father who sent me draws him"* (John 6:44). Stimulating spiritual hunger is ultimately a God thing. Apart from grace, *"there is no one who understands, no one who seeks God"* (Romans 3:11). It is God who opens our eyes to our need for Him. This being true, prayer is our primary means of arousing our children's interest in God. Pray like this:

> Dear God, stir in my child a desire for You. May my child hunger and thirst for You and respond quickly to Your invitation to come and be filled. (See Matthew 5:6; John 4:14.) Open his eyes to see You as You reveal yourself through Your Word and Spirit. Cause him to be aware of his need for You. Have mercy, Lord; please bring him to the end of himself without great distress—help him to reach out for someone beyond himself; cause him to reach out for You. In Jesus' wonderful name, Amen.

God is faithful to bring about circumstances in our children's lives that bring them to the end of their resources. It is only when we come to the end of ourselves that we reach for someone beyond. Our children are no different. They are inclined to hunger for God when they sense their need for help. Referring to the children of Israel, Moses recorded,

He humbled you, causing you to hunger and then feeding you with manna, which neither you nor your fathers had known, to teach you that man does not live on bread alone but on every word that comes from the mouth of the LORD.

(Deuteronomy 8:3)

6. Be Available

When the need arises, be there. God is faithful to provide times in your children's lives when they have no recourse but to cry out for Him. My daughter came to me in tears recently about a test she had failed. "I studied so hard. I feel so dumb," she wept. I held her in my arms and listened to her. I just let her spill out her pain. Then, I led her in a brief prayer: "Father, I feel like quitting. I can't do this stuff on my own anymore. I need You to help me. Take over, God." Peace immediately settled into her heart.

Reassuring hugs make great theology. Your loving support will soften your child's heart and open her up to God's love.

Reassuring hugs make great theology.

Take advantage of teachable moments. One of my daughters asked me not long ago, "Dad, I believe in God and everything, but how do I get close to Him?" Times like these are invaluable, but rarely convenient. I had several deadlines and appointments that day, but this was a moment that required my full attention. The best time to talk about God is anytime—yet occasions in which our kids really listen are rare. As much as possible, make yourself available for those golden, teachable moments. Talk to your children about the Lord as you sit, walk, lie down, and get up. (See Deuteronomy 6:7.)

Finally, be alert to your child's spiritual hunger and recognize its signs. Drop everything and be available to your child when he or she

- asks spiritual questions.
- reports unidentified guilt.
- prays longer and more in-depth.
- desires to go to church to worship.
- shows interest in the Bible.
- shows interest in giving.
- shows interest in baptism.

7. Use Discipline

Use the sorrow of discipline to stimulate a need for God. When consequences loom ominously on the horizon, a child is keenly aware of his need for help. The boy who threw a dirt bomb at his brother and broke a neighbor's thousand-dollar picture window is extremely conscious of his need for mercy and a financial miracle. It is at times like these that a child is apt to turn to a higher power. Painful consequences tend to humble us and bring about admission of our need for God.

Guilt may not be a pleasant emotion, but it is a big motivator. When a child is disciplined, encourage him to confess his transgression. Ask, "Bobby, what did you do that was wrong?" The weight of his guilt will hopefully produce a healthy sense of remorse and move your child to repent and seek forgiveness. Encourage him to pray, "Dear Jesus, I'm so sorry for the bad thing that I did. Please forgive me. In Your name, amen." Then assure your child that he is forgiven, and do not bring up the matter again.

8. Create a Need

Serve God together. Nothing generates a need for God more than getting in over your head. When kids are faced with needs that they do not have the resources to meet—when what they have is not enough to meet the needs of those who are hurting—they are inclined to reach out to God.

A family in Wisconsin organizes a family mission trip each year for their church. The father shared with me that these trips renew a passion for God in each family member:

> Something wonderful happens to the dynamics of a family when you have to work together and depend on each other to accomplish an important objective. You start to respect each other. You start to see each person as an individual. And when you see your youngest praying and depending on God to fix a broken transmission and God answers that prayer, you realize how God can work through each one of us.

Here are some suggestions for family mission and service projects:

- Helping in a soup kitchen
- Teaching a class together
- Playing in a worship band together
- Raking leaves for the elderly in your neighborhood
- Bringing meals to families in need
- Visiting and ministering in a nursing home
- Adopting a town board: bringing them coffee and pastries for their monthly board meetings
- Volunteering in a local mission such as a Christian drug rehab program, a rescue mission, the Salvation Army, Habitat for Humanity, or an inner-city mission organization
- Going on a foreign mission trip with a bona fide sending organization or setting up your own mission trip through your church, involving construction projects, puppet ministry, and/or street drama

9. Family Devotions

I hesitate to use the "D" word. Perhaps like me, you've tried to have devotions with your family and wound up shouting, "Sit down and pray or else!" Family devotions don't have to be family demolitions, not if they are based on the needs of each family member. In the good old days, when our kids were young and loved to curl up in my lap and have me read a picture Bible to them, devotions were a snap. My kids loved family Bible and prayer times—especially if it postponed their bedtime. Then they got older, and their interests became more refined. By this I mean everything suddenly got boring. I have used a wide variety of devotionals since our children entered their teen years and, frankly, all of them have flopped. But I haven't given up!

Family devotions don't have to be family demolitions—not if they are based on the needs of each family member.

Our best devotions tend to be spontaneous these days. Though we still pray before bed each evening, our most intimate times with God occur when a personal need arises. We may be prompted to pray and search the Scriptures because of a test the next day, a conflict with a friend or sibling, or a desire to know about the end times. Very often these times of prayer lead to profitable discussions. Here are some hints for conducting family devotions that maintain interest:

- Be led by the Spirit. Pray that God would guide you and your child to discuss things that are on His heart.

- Ask open-ended questions about God's involvement in your child's life, such as these: "How can God help you to handle your fear?" "How is God directing you in your decision?" "What do you think God wants you to do?" "How does He feel about dating?" "How did God help you with your problem?" "What does God's Word say about this issue?"

- When all are present, give everyone a chance to participate—even if it's just turning the pages of the Bible.

- If it's not working, don't quit—experiment with new formats, different times, and various curriculums.

- Reward right answers with affirmation or even small prizes. "Whoever can find a verse about forgiveness wins a stick of gum."

- When it's time to pray, model short and to-the-point prayers that your child can imitate. Try not to overwhelm your child with preach-praying.

- When children are young and perhaps reluctant to pray out loud, go around in a circle and pray one-word prayers. "Let's all thank Jesus for one thing He did for us today."

- Most importantly, keep it short. No longer than five minutes for preschoolers and no more than fifteen minutes for teens. A preacher was invited over to Junior's house for dinner and was asked to lead in grace for the meal. After the pastor shared a brief prayer, Junior smiled and said, "You don't pray so long when you're hungry, do you Pastor?"

10. Take Your Children on Location

One of Jesus' favorite teaching methods was to take His disciples to mountains, seashores, cities, and orchards where fig trees, wells, and stones served as object lessons. The world was His classroom.

Not long ago, I woke my kids up at five o'clock on a Saturday morning and took them to a quiet ocean bay. (We stopped to get donuts and hot cocoa along the way, of course.) The lobster fishermen were busily pulling in their pots. I read from the Bible about how Jesus called James and John to leave their nets and follow Him. I asked them, "What if you were a fisherman like those guys out there? What if you had a family to take care of, and Jesus told you to leave your boat and follow Him? What would you say? Would you leave everything to follow Him?" The seagulls called out overhead. The waves slapped the rocky shore. Then I read about Peter's reaction to Jesus' miraculous catch of fish and asked, "How would you feel if you were on that boat with Jesus and you saw all those fish? What would you say to Jesus?" The atmosphere was charged with excitement as the kids imagined these events. The Bible became real to them.

Here is a short list of places you can go with your children to make God's Word come alive.

- Field: Read the story of the feeding of the five thousand. (See, for example Matthew 14:14–21; Luke 9:11–17.)
- Hill: Read the Sermon on the Mount. (See Matthew 5–7.)
- Country road: Read the story of Paul's journey on the road to Damascus (see Acts 9:1–20) or the two disciples on the road to Emmaus. (See Luke 24:13–34.)
- Orchard: Read the story of Jesus praying in the garden of Gethsemane (this garden was actually an olive orchard). (See Matthew 26:36–50; Mark 14:32–46.)
- Near a flock of sheep: Read John 10, and talk about how Jesus is the Good Shepherd and we are His sheep. Notice the characteristics of sheep.
- Ocean or lake: Read the events in Jesus' life that took place at the Sea of Galilee, such as the story of Jesus calming the storm. (See, for example, Mark 4:35–41.)
- Prison: Read the parable of the unmerciful servant who, because of his unforgiveness, wound up in jail. (See Matthew 18:22–35.)
- Hand-dug well: Read about the woman at the well. (See John 4:4–42.)

- Cemetery: Take your older children to a family member's grave and read the story of Lazarus, the resurrection of Jesus, or Paul's reference to the resurrection of believers. (See John 11:1–44; Matthew 28; Mark 16; Luke 24; John 20–21; 1 Thessalonians 4:13–18.)

One adventurous youth pastor took his Sunday school class to a graveyard on Easter morning. He read the story of the resurrection beside a mausoleum. An event that took place 2,000 years ago came alive to a group of forty teens. Many were touched by the reality of the resurrection that Easter.

11. Build a Secret Place for the Most High (Psalm 139:15)

Children think in concrete terms. By decorating a special place for children to meet with God, parents generate excitement and anticipation.

A friend's five-year-old son asked me if I wanted to go to his church. I thought he meant his father's church, since the boy's father was a pastor, until he took me by the hand and walked me out to a row of pine trees that shaded a corner of the family's fenced yard. "Under these trees is my church," the boy said proudly, "and I am the pastor." Later my friend told me his son prays, sings, and preaches to stuffed animals and neighborhood friends under the canopy of the trees. This little boy had made for himself a secret place for the Most High.

Encourage your child to find a closet, a corner of his room, or a tree fort that he can call his secret place with God. Allow him to decorate his spot in ways he feels will please the Lord (Christian posters, pictures, Bibles, cards, mementos). With your child's assistance, you may want to anoint the area with olive oil (a light touch in each corner), and explain that anointing oil sets a person, place, or thing apart for God. (See Leviticus 21:10–12; Exodus 30:26–30.) Take your child to his special place of worship whenever you want to pray with him or sing a worship song. A secret place will help God to become more real and personal to your child.

12. Emphasize the Taste, Not the Table Manners

Table manners have little meaning if no one wants to eat. Children are interested in personal holiness and the disciplines of the faith only after they discover how good God is. Cultivating a heartfelt love for God should be our top priority, not ensuring correct behavior. Proverbs reminds us, *"Above all else, guard your heart, for it is the wellspring of life"* (Proverbs 4:23).

Who wants to spend time with a Father whose only concern is whether or not his kids keep the rules?

Sarah (eight) was the last one in the van on Sunday morning. "What took you so long?" her mother asked. "I was getting my Bible," she said. Her mother had tried to get Sarah to remember to bring her Bible to church for years. "What made you remember?" her mother queried. "I think it makes Jesus happy," was Sarah's reply.

Sarah's newfound habit was a matter of the heart, not her mother's harangue. She was motivated to bring her Bible because she wanted to please God.

Parents who insist that their children maintain rigid religious standards but fail to acquaint them with the joy of simply knowing Jesus, introduce their children to the taste of legalism, not the taste of God. Hearing only the "oughts," "musts," and "shoulds" of the Christian faith is not too appetizing. Shame and guilt can, in fact, ruin a healthy spiritual appetite. Who wants to spend time with a Father whose only concern is whether or not His kids keep the rules?

One morning I got frustrated with my children because they weren't coming downstairs fast enough for our family quiet time. My schedule was extremely demanding that day, and I wanted to get this show on the road. When there was still no response from the upstairs after the third call, I decided to take action. I yelled. I threatened. I criticized. And I got results. Not the results I really wanted, however. I had two children and a wife at the table, Bibles in hand—upset, hurt, and angry. As I opened in prayer, the whole thing seemed ludicrous. Gritting my teeth, I prayed, "Dear Jesus, thank You for this wonderful day. Help us to hear from You today in our quiet time..." I broke off my prayer and looked into the sullen eyes of my wife and children. The only passion I had cultivated in their hearts was resentment. For our family devotions that morning, I taught on humility and repentance—I made a great object lesson.

How can you avoid an undue emphasis on behavior and rules?

- Be aware of your motives for serving God. If you seek God to gain recognition, acceptance, or forgiveness, you probably place a greater concern on what you should do rather than what God has done.
- Attend a church that is more concerned about transforming the inner man than conforming the outer man. (See Romans 12:2; Ephesians 3:16.) Legalism focuses on good behavior rather than the motivation for good behavior. Whereas God judges the heart of a man, legalism judges appearance and performance. Because children are naturally concerned with pleasing others with their behavior and performance, they are especially at risk for internalizing legalistic attitudes and therefore need to be sheltered from environments that offer a steady diet of rule keeping. Legalism is like yeast, the apostle Paul says, in that it *works through the whole batch of dough* (1 Corinthians 5:6).
- Keep your expectations realistic. Henrietta Mears, renowned Christian educator of the early twentieth century, said this

about teaching kids: "God put that wiggle in your child. Don't try to take it out!" Let your child be a child. Children are quick to move from praying to playing and are intensely sincere about both. They will probably not describe an encounter with God as "a glorious time in the Lord." One eight-year-old in our church described his experience with God in this way, "Wow! That was so cool!"

- Focus on your children's motivation, not solely on their behavior. Help them to understand why they do what they do. Instead of, "Jeremy, don't say that about your sister! You know that's a sin!" ask him, "Jeremy, you hurt your sister's feelings. It's not like you. What were you feeling? What were you thinking? How can God help you?" Rather than, "Lisa, you know better than to watch that TV show. Go to your room," ask, "Lisa, can you tell me how this program will help you to get closer to God? What are the values of this show? Do they make God happy or sad?" Rather than giving your child a list of "oughts," help your child to understand why obedience is a good idea. Help your daughter see why bringing her Walkman to church is not a good idea by asking her, "Debbie, what is the reason we go to church? Will your Walkman help you to achieve that purpose?" as opposed to, "Debbie, you can't bring your Walkman to church. It's just not right."

- Emphasize the "get to's" of the Bible. Avoid a heavy and oppressive climate in your home by not letting the "don'ts" of faith training outweigh the "can's." Be positive. Teach your children that they *get to* please the God of the universe through their good behavior; *get to* serve God and make a difference in church and at home; *get to* pray and see God move; *get to* tell others about Jesus so that they can spend eternity in heaven.

13. Give Them a Cone of Their Own

A mother called her son into the kitchen and said, "Stevie, last night there were two pints of ice cream in the freezer, and now there is only one. Can you explain that?" "Yes, Mama," the boy replied innocently. "I guess I just didn't see the other pint!" This boy wanted a double portion!

Once hunger is aroused, it's time to give our children their own servings. After one taste, they will want more! Leading your child to Christ is an amazing and wonderful experience. No technical skill is needed. If Jesus is living in you, you have everything you need.

People ask me, "When are my children ready to receive Christ?" I tell them, without trying to be facetious, "They are ready when they are ready." When your daughter wants to receive Christ, don't deny her. Lead her to Christ. There is certainly no harm in leading your child to Christ over and over until she grasps a more solid understanding of the gospel and its holding power. Encourage your child to pray something like this:

"Jesus, I give You my heart."

"Jesus, I give You my life."

"Jesus, please be my best Friend."

"I will obey You, Jesus."

These are all wonderful responses to God's invitation, *"If anyone is thirsty, let him come to me and drink"* (John 7:37).

After the age of seven, most children can grasp the full meaning of the gospel (Christ's substitutionary death and atonement) and have a greater understanding of their own moral condition. During this time, a child is capable of what we call conversion. The following prayer may be helpful to parents who seek to lead their elementary children into a salvation experience.

Dear Jesus, thank You for dying for me on the cross. You were punished for all the bad things I've done. Please forgive me for the times I've done bad things. Come into my heart and help me to obey You. Thank You for being my best Friend and for being with me forever. I love You. In Jesus' name, Amen.

How do we know when our children are ready for true conversion (ready to be saved)? Here some indicators:

- Your child shows an unusual interest in the Bible, Sunday school, and/or worship songs.
- He/she persistently asks questions about baptism, God, sin, heaven, and/or hell.
- He/she exhibits an intense desire to go to church, listen to Christian music, and help out in serving around the house.
- He/she is concerned about his/her eternal destination.
- He/she is curious about the meaning of certain biblical terms, like saved, salvation, repentance, and atonement. One little girl simply asked her mother, "Mommy, what does it mean to be 'saved'?"
- He/she feels unusually sorry for his/her misbehavior.
- He/she becomes nervous and agitated when you talk about God—as if he/she knows he/she should respond to God in a certain way but does not know how.
- When you pray with him/her, he/she wants to express himself/herself to God but has difficulty.

What about those kids who were raised in the faith and seem to be already saved? Children who have been raised in homes permeated with the love and presence of God often seem to have simply assimilated Jesus into their hearts. Asking them to receive Christ as Lord and Savior seems superfluous and somewhat artificial. It seems more appropriate to ask if they would like Jesus to stay, rather than to come! Though children may clearly demonstrate evidence of being saved, I still recommend leading them to Christ through formal prayer. Having a specific date of conversion serves as a lifelong reference point for their decision to follow Jesus.

Though a genuine conversion experience may need to wait until a child is older, children are ready at any age to enjoy the joy and peace of God's presence. Jesus said, *"Let the little children come to me"* (Matthew 19:14). No matter what level of cognitive and moral development your child is at, Jesus wants to initiate a relationship with him. The apostle Paul wrote that Timothy was instructed in Scripture from infancy! (See 2 Timothy 3:14–15.) We can introduce our children to God's presence as we pray for them in their cribs and hold them in our arms when we worship; kids of all ages appreciate God's Spirit. As the prophet Joel said, *"I will pour out my Spirit on all people. Your sons and daughters will prophesy"* (Joel 2:28).

A Sunday school teacher asked her class to take some time on Sunday afternoon to write a letter to God about their experience at church. One little boy wrote, "Dear God, We had a pretty good time at church today. Wish You could have been there."

God forbid that we give our children meaningless ritual, dry doctrine, and laws and rules, instead of a living relationship. Our children crave a real experience with God. May God help us to introduce our children to the person of Jesus so that they taste and see that He is good and want more for themselves.

Chapter Notes

1. Saint Augustine, *The Confessions of Saint Augustine* (New Kensington, Pa.: Whitaker House, 1996), 11.

2. Gloria Gaither, *What My Parents Did Right!* (West Monroe, La.: Howard Publishing Co., Inc., 2002), 239–240.

3. Daniel Okrent, "Raising Kids Online," *Time*, May 10, 1999.

4. Blakely Bundy, M.Ed., "How to Get Kids Off TV," *Bottom Line/Personal*, February 1, 1997, 13. <http://www.bottomlinesecrets.com/blpnet/article.html?article_id=8106> (January 13, 2006)

5. "Teen and Drugs Fast Facts," National Drug Intelligence Center. <http://www.usdoj.gov/ndic/pubs11/12430/index.htm> (January 10, 2006)

CHAPTER 14

Praying on Purpose

THE WAR AGAINST THE HOME

A little girl was praying up a storm one night. She concluded by asking God, "Before I finish, dear Lord, please take care of Daddy, take care of Mommy, take care of my baby brother...and please, God, take care of Yourself, or else we're all sunk!"

She's right! God is our only hope against the spiritual forces that seek to destroy our families. Children are the targets of pornographers and drug dealers, the casualties of marital conflict, and the victims of teen suicide and child abuse.

Homes continue to be shattered by divorce at a steady rate of about 49 percent of all new marriages, and Christian marriages are not immune. Around 85,500 children experience the breakup of their parents' marriages every month.[1] Children of divorce show a tendency toward depression, excessive guilt, underachievement, uncontrolled anger, and an inability to form intimate relationships.

Parents prone to act out of their own woundedness are likely to lash out at their children in anger and perpetuate emotional scarring in the next generation. According to a study conducted by the Family Research Lab at the University of New Hampshire, by the time a child reaches seven years old, 98 percent of parents are verbally lashing out.

One out of five parents has threatened to kick a teenage son or daughter out of the house, while a quarter has sworn at their offspring. In a previous study, verbal aggressiveness among parents accounted for a wide range of childhood woes: depression, eating disorders, and delinquency.[2]

Trends like these suggest that there is a conspiracy underway to destroy the emotional and spiritual well-being of children. Conspiracy is not too strong a word. A demonic assault is being launched upon the next generation of believers—principally the next generation of Christian kids.

Our mortal enemy knows that if he can wound our children emotionally, he can lead them into sinful and self-destructive methods of managing their needs. His ultimate goal is to destroy their destinies and the destinies of their children. He must eliminate all threats to his hold on this earth. Our deep-rooted sin patterns play right into his plan.

> A demonic assault is being launched upon the next generation of Christian kids.

His attack upon the family does not go unchallenged, however. God said to Satan, *"And I will put enmity between you and the woman, and between your offspring and hers"* (Genesis 3:15). In effect, God declared war on the forces of hell.

The Bible also says that this war is already won. Christ defeated the devil at the cross: *"...he [Christ] will crush your head, and you will strike his heel"* (Genesis 3:15). *"And having disarmed the powers and authorities, he [Christ] made a public spectacle of them, triumphing over them by the cross"* (Colossians 2:15).

Though the church is assured ultimate victory, the war is far from over. The devil is determined to inflict as much harm upon the next generation as he can before his time is up. Our family members are at stake. Unless we stand up and fight for them, they will become casualties of war.

In combat there is no neutral ground; you either fight to defend those you love, or you surrender them to the enemy. You are either victorious, or your loved ones are taken prisoner and/or killed.

Many parents are ignorant of the fact that their homes are under siege. They are preoccupied with personal needs and unaware that spiritual powers seek to enslave their children. Some receive a rude awakening when they discover serious sin in their child's life. They wonder how such a thing could have happened to their family.

Others are aware that they are engaged in a spiritual battle but depend on faulty weapons to defend their family. They believe that by teaching, correcting, and advising their children, they can protect them from the ravages of the devil. But no amount of moral training can stop the devil from destroying a child. I know young people who have more Christian character than most, but are far from God and ineffective in the kingdom. No amount of human effort will win a spiritual battle.

> *Unless we stand up and fight for our family members, they will become casualties of war and we will have to surrender them to the enemy.*

WINNING THE WAR

Paul tells us that, though we are powerless in our own strength to win the battle for our children's souls, we have divine power through prayer!

The weapons we fight with are not the weapons of the world. On the contrary, they have divine power to demolish strongholds.

(2 Corinthians 10:4)

Bob often felt helpless in his desire to lead his son to Christ. His son lived out of state with his mother, and he saw the boy only two weeks out of the year. All Bob could do was pray.

> I started praying. I prayed that everything that happened in his life God would turn around for His honor and praise. I prayed that God would raise him up to be a "Soldier of Christ," and that somehow, he'd find some kind of Christian influence where he was living.

One night Bob got a call from his son. "Guess what, Dad? I became a Christian!" Much to Bob's surprise, his son had made several Christian friends at school and had been going to youth groups at two different churches.

Prayer destroys the devil's plans to capture the hearts of our children. *"The reason the Son of God appeared was to destroy the devil's work"* (1 John 3:8). We must learn to fight in prayer for the souls of our children. Pray in this way:

1. **Passionately.** Much is at stake. The Bible indicates that the devil prowls about like a roaring lion seeking defenseless victims to devour. (See 1 Peter 5:8.) Your children are in danger. God has given you the responsibility to protect them through prayer.

2. **Personally.** Pray that God would set you free from behaviors that wound your children. We want to inspire trust and model the Father's love.

3. **Specifically.** Ask God to protect each of your children from anything that would keep them from embracing God's plan for their lives. Pray that, as your children grow up, the only wounds and scars they would know would be those of Jesus. Ask Him to cause your children's hearts to yearn for His presence and that they would be fully able to appropriate His love.

4. **Expectantly.** Pray that your child's future spouse and children would be protected and preserved. Ask God to help your child's future in-laws to raise their son or daughter in a way that is free from spiritual, emotional, and physical scars. Ask God to open the doors of your child's destiny so that every opportunity for training and experience is available. Pray that your grandchildren would love God with all their hearts.

5. **Faithfully.** Bring your children before the Lord each day for His protection and provision. His mercies are new every morning. Great is His faithfulness to our children. (See Lamentations 3:23.)

WARFARE PRAYER FOR OUR CHILDREN

Father, the devil wants to destroy my child. You know this better than I do. In the power and authority of Jesus Christ, Your Son, I crush the devil's plan to rob my child of his/her calling and to control his/her life with fear, crippling insecurity, and self-destructive attitudes and behaviors. In the power and authority of Jesus Christ, whom You raised from the dead and seated beside Your right hand, I tear down and smash all strongholds of rebellion, negativity, hopelessness, and resentment in his/her life. In Your power, I destroy the temptation of drugs, alcohol, cigarettes, pornography, and promiscuity in his/her life.

I smash and destroy the devil's scheme to destroy my child's capacity to trust—a scheme intended to make depending on You more difficult. In Your strength, I will be a trustworthy and safe parent. I will meet my child's emotional needs and I will reinforce my child's ability to trust. Reveal to me areas of my life that need healing. Don't let me give the devil a foothold from which to work his plan to destroy my family. Show me where I am wounded, and heal me, so that I will not wound my spouse and children. Set me free to model Your love, Lord. Don't allow me to pass on my generational junk. Stop the cycle in this generation!

Father, if I have already wounded my family, forgive me. Help me to seek forgiveness from my spouse and children. Please give my child the grace he/she needs to forgive me and to restore his/her faith in me. Don't let my child develop sinful ways of managing his/her own unmet needs. Heal his/her heart. In the authority of Your name, I tear down the devil's plan to get my child to rely on counterfeit forms of love and security to gain worth and value.

Father, protect my child from temptations that are too great for him/her to handle. Help me to be alert to cultural and peer influences that would seduce him/her away from You. Give me discernment to know when a media message or a peer relationship is too powerful for him/her to resist.

I pray that You would give my child a greater hunger for You. Cause my child to want You with all his/her heart. May his/her heart burn for You, Lord. May it burn with an ever growing fire for You. Create circumstances in his/her life that will turn him/her to You—may he/she settle for nothing less than all of You.

I pray that my child would fulfill every aspect of his/her calling. Help my child to know his/her gifts and passion and to grow in them. In Your power, I come against discouragement, despair, and fear in his/her life. Encourage my child by Your Spirit. Cause him/her to want to be well trained in his/her calling. Give my child determination to complete the work You have for him/her.

I pray that You would lead my child to his/her spouse, Lord. Protect his/her future mate from emotional, spiritual, and physical scars. Guide my child's spouse into his/her calling, and may it complement my child's. May they serve You together and complete the purposes You have ordained for them as a couple.

Help my child to be pure and to make the most of his/her single years. Help my child to be content and to wait for You to bring him/her a mate for life.

I pray for my grandchildren, Lord, that they would fulfill their callings and would love You with all their hearts.

Thank You for allowing me the privilege to raise a child on purpose, God. In Jesus' name, Amen.

Former U.S. Attorney General John Ashcroft tells a story of how his father's dependence on prayer left a memorable impression on him during his inauguration as U.S. Senator from Missouri. Just before he was sworn in, a group of friends and family assembled around John to pray. Among them was his elderly father, who had accompanied him to Washington, D.C., to watch the event. The newly elected senator noticed his father trying to get up off the sofa to join the group. Turning to his father, he said, "Dad, you don't have to struggle to stand." His father replied weakly but with clarity, "Son, I'm not struggling to stand; I'm struggling to kneel."

"That day," says Mr. Ashcroft, "was the last day of my father's life. He died on his way returning home to Missouri. If you can freeze that frame for a moment—an ailing, aged father not struggling to stand but struggling to kneel and pray beside his kneeling son—you can observe a picture of what will help save America."[3]

Chapter Notes

1. Mary Darby, "Christian Self-esteem," *Home Life*, January 1992, 2.
2. Rachel K. Sobel, "Wounding with Words," *U.S. News & World Report*, August 28, 2000, 53.
3. John Ashcroft, *Intercessors for America Newsletter*, December 1995, 3.

CHAPTER 15

Making History in Our Homes

O ur parenting will change the world! What a claim to make, especially when many of us are simply trying to find the energy to get off the couch and change the baby's diaper. Yet it's true. Our parenting, for better or for worse, will change the world. One hundred and fifty years ago, Abraham Lincoln said this about children:

> A child is a person who is going to carry on what you have started....He will assume control of your cities, states, and nations. He is going to move in and take over your churches, schools, universities, and corporations. The fate of humanity is in his hands.

Not long from now, our kids will assume responsibility for our nations and churches. Will they bring positive change? Of particular concern to us, will they establish God's purposes for their generation? To a large extent, the answer depends on whether we raise them on purpose—their God-given purpose.

Consider Abraham and Sarah. By raising their son on purpose, they blessed the whole world for all time!

Abraham and Sarah understood that Isaac was born for a divine purpose—to transfer the promises of God to the next generation. They embraced their responsibility to parent on purpose and gave rise to a nation of sons and daughters who shared the covenant promises of

God with all nations. Their descendants would even bring forth the Messiah—Jesus, the Savior of the world. Through their parenting, the whole earth was blessed!

> *And you are heirs of the prophets and of the covenant God made with your fathers. He said to Abraham, Through your offspring all peoples on earth will be blessed.* (Acts 3:25)

God saw in Abraham's DNA a father who would recognize his son's calling and equip him to fulfill it. God chose him to be the father of His people because He knew Abraham would train up his children in the way that they should go.

> *For I have chosen him, so that he will direct his children and his household after him to keep the way of the LORD by doing what is right and just, so that the LORD will bring about for Abraham what he has promised him.* (Genesis 18:19)

Eight hundred years later, in a little town called Bethlehem, God chose two more parents (offspring of Abraham and Sarah) to make redemptive history. God didn't send His Son into the world riding down Jerusalem Avenue in a flaming chariot, nor did He "beam" Him into Herod's palace as a thirty-year-old adult. Instead, He sent His Son as a vulnerable, dependent child and entrusted His care to two fallible human beings. Why? Because He knew Joseph and Mary would raise Him on purpose—a purpose that would ultimately change the course of history.

> *Then Simeon blessed them and said to Mary, his mother: "This child is destined to cause the falling and rising of many in Israel, and to be a sign that will be spoken against, so that the thoughts of many hearts will be revealed. And a sword will pierce your own soul too."* (Luke 2:34–35)

Parenting can change the world. Scripture reveals that every great move of God was prefigured by the birth of a child. The birth of Isaac anticipated the formation of a people of God. The arrival of Moses signaled an age of deliverance. John the Baptist heralded an age of repentance. The advent of Jesus proclaimed that the kingdom of God had come to earth. These children would grow up to usher in God's unique purposes for their generations. They could not fulfill their destinies alone, however. They needed parents who recognized their distinctive callings and facilitated them. God is counting on us to advance His kingdom through our children as well.

Jonathan Edwards, the American revivalist and theologian of the first Great Awakening, is another example of how parents can make redemptive history. Out of his 1,394 descendants, thirteen were college presidents, sixty-five were professors, sixty were prominent lawyers, thirty-two were noted authors, ninety were physicians, two hundred were gospel-preaching ministers, and three hundred were good farmers.[1] How true the Word of God is when it says, *"The righteous man leads a blameless life; blessed are his children after him"* (Proverbs 20:7).

> *Our parenting, for better or worse, will change the world.*

Like Jonathan Edwards, we are to leave legacies of sons and daughters who will impact their generation with the purposes of God.

> *Tell it to your children, and let your children tell it to their children, and their children to the next generation.*   (Joel 1:3)

Parenting on purpose starts with the end in mind. Simply put, it discovers the way a child is to go and helps him to get there. Many years ago, while eating lunch at a Chinese restaurant, my daughter Rachael, three at the time, asked me a question that opened my eyes to my purpose for parenting. At the end of the meal, she handed me her fortune cookie and asked, "Daddy, can you please help me get my fortune?"

As I looked into her big, brown eyes, it was like a bell went off: "That's it! That's my job! I'm supposed to help her find God's fortune—her calling, her destiny." It is our distinct privilege as parents to help our children discover their purposes in life. We are to raise our children on purpose—to help them find the way they should go and to enter it. (See Proverbs 22:6.)

Using the DNA Analysis Survey, astute observation, and prayer, we can help our children identify their God-given gifts and passions. With this information in hand, we can assist our children to prayerfully surmise their general direction in life—"the way they are to go."

Yet what good is knowing the way our children are to go, if they don't want to go there? Remember that recognizing our children's unique, God-given way is only the starting point. In order to fulfill their destinies, our kids must love God with all their hearts and passionately seek their callings.

> Not long from now, our kids will assume responsibility for our churches and nations.

How do we cultivate a passion for Jesus? Again, by warming their hearts, we kindle a fire for God. Faithfully meeting our children's emotional needs for protection, acceptance, recognition, enforced limits, nearness, time, and support, we develop within their hearts a capacity to manage their needs through dependence on God and others. Children look to us to meet their emotional ("PARENTS") needs. As we faithfully respond, they see the reasonableness of relying on others to meet their needs. This ability to trust constitutes the emotional groundwork required for a vibrant and enduring faith in God.

In contrast, children who were disappointed and hurt as they looked to their parents for recognition, security, and support view trust as a setup for more heartache. Trusting others—even God—is extremely difficult for those from homes like these. Frequently, when trust has been damaged in childhood, children grow up resorting to manipulation and control to meet their needs.

Meeting our children's emotional needs inspires a love for God in another way as well. As we faithfully love and protect our children, we model the Father's love and help them to form an accurate perception of God's character. Kids can generally perceive in God only what they have received from us. The better a parent represents God's care, the better chance a child has to internalize an accurate image of God. The way our children perceive God determines the way they will respond to Him.

Parents who meet their children's emotional needs lay a foundation for destiny. Children grow up emotionally secure, undistracted by unmet emotional needs, and able to see God for who He really is.

Finally, one thing is still needed for our children to pursue God. Our children must meet Him. It's not enough to know about God; children need a living relationship to fulfill their destinies. By modeling our love

> *The better a parent represents God's care, the better chance a child has to internalize an accurate image of Him.*

for God, we whet their spiritual appetites. Once they show personal interest, we can introduce them to Christ.

The most important thing we can do to raise our children on purpose is to pray on purpose. The devil has a plan of his own for our children—a plan to enslave them and to destroy their redeeming influence upon this world. We are at war. We must fight to preserve and protect our children through prayer.

Appendix L, "Becoming Parents of Destiny Checklist," provides you with a way to regularly examine where you are in enabling your children to full their God-given callings.

It's hard to see how our parenting has the potential to change the world when a pile of dirty laundry blocks our view. The demands of daily life keep most of us completely tied up in the present. Regardless of what we see now, however, our parenting will largely determine the condition of the world twenty years from now. Centuries ago, author Otto Brunfel said it well:

> For what more Christian thing could happen than that children be raised well and taught self-discipline, useable skills, and a sense of honor? What richer and better inheritance could any father give his children? If one wants to reform the world and make it Christian, one must begin with children.

> *I will open my mouth in parables, I will utter hidden things, things from of old—what we have heard and known, what our fathers have told us. We will not hide them from their children; we will tell the next generation the praiseworthy deeds of the LORD, his power, and the wonders he has done. He decreed statutes for Jacob and established the law in Israel, which he commanded our forefathers to teach their children, so the next generation would know them, even the children yet to be born, and they in turn would tell their children. Then they would put their trust in God and would not forget his deeds but would keep his commands.* (Psalm 78:2–7)

By raising your children on purpose—their God-given purpose—you make redemptive history and impact the generations to come for the cause of Christ.

You make history in your home.

But the plans of the LORD stand firm forever, the purposes of his heart through all generations. (Psalm 33:11)

Chapter Notes

1. <http://elbourne.org/sermons/index.mv?illustration+4325> (November 10, 2005)

A Prayer to Parent on Purpose

Father,

Help me to raise my children on purpose.

You formed their DNA—their Divine Notion Awaiting. Help me to raise them to fulfill it.

Help me to recognize the individual gifts and unique desires You've placed within my children so that I might raise them according to the way they should go. Allow me the privilege to raise them to enter Your plan for their lives so that Your purposes may be released in their generation.

Give me the love I need to meet their emotional needs. Help me to develop their capacity to trust so that they may give themselves away to You someday. Help me to model Your love to them, as well, so that they see Your love and one day want more.

Lord, lead my children's future spouses to You. Help them to be good parents to my grandchildren. Lead them to enter into Your purposes for their lives, early in life.

Finally, Lord, I pray for my grandchildren. Protect them and keep them close to You all the days of their lives. Use them to take Your purposes to their generation. Make them history makers and world changers!

In Jesus' name, Amen.

Appendices

APPENDIX A

Taking a "DNA" Survey:

THE DESTINY SURVEY CHART

The Destiny Survey Chart illustrates how calling is found where gifting and spiritual passion intersect. This visual aid is helpful for explaining to children the concept of spiritual DNA. The chart also includes questions children may ask themselves, their friends, and mentors to gain information about their callings.

In the box below is a biblical basis for the Destiny Survey Chart. Children may use these statements as scriptural affirmations for their lives and callings.

I am called to serve God in ways that express my unique gifts and special interests. (1 Corinthians 12)

1. God has a special plan for my life—a "way" for me to go. (See Proverbs 22:6.)
2. God created me for a special purpose. (See Psalm 139:15–16.)
3. The apostle Paul said that I was created to do good works—I have a job to do for God. (See Ephesians 2:10.)
4. These good works are expressed through unique gifting(s) that God put inside me according to His Spirit, and are for the benefit of the purposes of God's kingdom. (See 1 Corinthians 12.)
5. The unique gifts and interests that made up God's plan for David's life were seen in his youth. (See 1 Samuel 17:32–52.)
6. Jeremiah felt that he was too young to speak for God until God told him that he was called to be a prophet before he was even born. (See Jeremiah 1:6.)
7. Esther had to overcome fear to fulfill her destiny. (See Esther 4:10–16.)

Destiny Survey Chart

This is the way; walk in it. —Isaiah 30:21 (NIV)

God-given Gifts*

- _____
- _____
- _____
- _____
- _____

My Purpose & Calling

≈ ≈ ≈

Spiritual "DNA"

God-given Passions*

- _____
- _____
- _____
- _____
- _____

What are my special gifts?
What have I been recognized for?
What activities do I do well in?
What do my peers/mentors see in me?

What are my unique interests?
What do I like to do?
What would I be willing to do for free?
What captivates my imagination?

*Gifts: what we do well (talents)

*Passions: what we like to do

☙ Discover God's Plan for Your Future ☙

Interview Questions to Ask the Child and Friends, Parents, Teachers, and Mentors

1. What do I love doing for God?
2. What would I do for God if money were no object?
3. What am I good at?
4. What captures my imagination?
5. What skills and talents do you see in me that are unique? (gifting)
6. What do others seek from me or look for me to do? (gifting)
7. How do I positively affect others?
8. In what ways do I bring positive change?
9. What kind of people do I like to help and serve? (passion)

Personality Plays a Part:

FOUR-TEMPERAMENT MODEL
OF HUMAN BEHAVIOR

A long with determining gifting and spiritual passion, identifying a child's unique personality can help determine God's plan for his life. God has given your child a unique personality profile that is perfectly designed for his calling.

The graph on the next page illustrates the classic Four-Temperament Model of Human Behavior. To identify your child's profile, compare his social and task-related qualities to those listed in each quadrant.

Four-Temperament Model of Human Behavior

This is the way; walk in it. —Isaiah 30:21 (NIV)

RELATIONSHIP-ORIENTED
(gives higher value to relationships, lower value to results)

OUTGOING
(higher outgoing style, lower contemplative style)

RESERVED
(higher contemplative style, lower outgoing style)

Sammy Census

Biblical Example: Peter

Qualities:
friendly, social, dreamy,
carefree, talkative, restless,
impulsive, undisciplined

Susie Standbyu

Biblical Example: Abraham

Qualities:
dependable, calm, sensitive,
supportive, easygoing,
fearful, noncommittal

Jamie Justdoit

Biblical Example: Paul

Qualities:
independent, forceful,
practical, determined,
optimistic, demanding,
intimidating

Randy Right

Biblical Example: Moses

Qualities:
analytical, thorough,
perfectionistic, careful,
critical, negative, rigid,
closed-minded

RESULTS-ORIENTED
(gives higher value to results, lower value to relationships)

Discovering My Story

U se this chart to summarize and compare your children's gifts, passions, and temperament (personality). Review this information with your children and encourage them to recognize how God has created them to fulfill a special purpose. As your children begin to understand that they are called to serve, explore various vocations with them. (See Appendix D.)

Discovering My Story

This is the way; walk in it. —Isaiah 30:21 (NIV)

God-given Passions

What do you love to do?

_____
_____
_____

God-given Gifts

What do you love to do for others?

_____
_____
_____

God-given Purpose & Calling

Spiritual "DNA"

God-given Temperament

How do you relate to others and to the world? As...

1. Sammy Census
2. Susie Standbyu
3. Jamie Justdoit
4. Randy Right

History of Achievements

What have I done in the past that has been recognized?

List awards and honors received...

As a Preschooler • In Elementary School

During Middle School • In High School

During College/Grad School • As an Adult

RESERVED

RELATIONSHIP-ORIENTED

Susie Standbyu

Randy Right

RESULTS-ORIENTED

Sammy Census

Jamie Justdoit

OUTGOING

Identifying Vocation Based on Gifts, Passion, and Temperament

Review the following list of possible vocations for your children based on their gifts, spiritual passions, and temperaments. (This is not an exhaustive list, but will give you a starting place for exploring potential vocations.) Note also how vocation and personality intersect, as shown in the Four-Temperament Model with Vocation Options chart.

Artistic Jobs
Animator (cartoons and films)
Musician
Film Editor
Actor
Graphic Designer
Clothes, Fabric, Decorating Designer
Fiction Writer
Photographer

Jobs That Help People Learn
Elementary or High School Teacher
Professor (Teacher of Older People in College)
Special Education Teacher
Counselor
Reading Specialist
Librarian
Reporter
Non-fiction Writer
Youth or Children's Minister
Pastor

Jobs That Help People to Stop Hurting/Be Healthy
Physician
Nurse
X-ray Technician
Chiropractor
Physical Therapist
Dentist
Optometrist
Dermatologist
Psychiatrist
Pharmacist
Nutritionist

Jobs That Help and Protect People
Police Officer
Soldier
Firefighter
EMS (Emergency Medical Service)
Lawyer
Government Leader or Politician
Diplomat

Jobs That Work with Numbers and Build or Fix Things
Computer Technician
Mechanic
Engineer or other Technologist
Inventor
Scientist

Jobs That Work with Numbers and Generate Business/Help People
Accountant
Salesperson
Businessperson
Business Starter (Entrepreneur)
Insurance Agent
Financial Planner

Jobs That Use Your Hands
Driver
Pilot
Chef
Repairperson
Painter
Custodian
Industrial Worker

<u>Jobs in Sports</u>
Fitness Trainer
Player
Coach
Manager
Sports writer

Note: A great career/vocational resource for children and parents is "Pandora's Briefcase: A Kid's Guide to Careers," from ThinkQuest. You can access it through the following URL: http://www.thinkquest.org/library/site.html?team_id=J001784.

4-Temperament Model
with Vocation Options

RELATIONSHIP-ORIENTED
(gives higher value to relationships, lower value to results)

OUTGOING
(higher outgoing style, lower contemplative style)

RESERVED
(higher contemplative style, lower outgoing style)

RESULTS-ORIENTED
(gives higher value to results, lower value to relationships)

Sammy Census

Biblical Example: Peter

Sample Vocations:
salesperson, teacher, speaker, customer serviceperson

Susie Standbyu

Biblical Example: Abraham

Sample Vocations:
counselor, diplomat, administrative assistant

Jamie Justdoit

Biblical Example: Paul

Sample Vocations:
contractor, business owner, director

Randy Right

Biblical Example: Moses

Sample Vocations:
lawyer, engineer, accountant, artist

Breaking the Cycle Worksheet

ADDITIONAL PARENTING HELP FOR THOSE FROM
LESS-THAN-IDEAL HOMES

We can only give our children what we have received. If we experienced respect, understanding, and affirmation growing up, we have a context for giving and receiving love today. If we were put down and made fun of, humiliated for sharing our needs, or disciplined in ways that shamed us, our concept and expression of love is probably skewed and, unless corrected, likely to be passed on to our children. We will treat our children the way we were treated—for better and for worse.

Giving our children the love they need means we must receive it first. How do we break the cycle? Our Father in heaven offers us the opportunity to be born into the arms of a perfect Parent and to be re-parented in His perfect love. As we allow God to love us in ways we have always needed, our hearts will be filled with the kind of love our children need. Out of His abundant love toward us, we may love abundantly. *"Dear friends, since God so loved us, we also ought to love one another"* (1 John 4:11).

To ensure your children are receiving the kind of love they need, take the survey on page 200 entitled "How Am I Meeting My Children's Needs?" Then, ask your spouse and children for feedback about your parenting using the second survey, "How Does My Family Feel I Am Meeting Their Needs?" You might also ask them additional questions, such as "What do I do that makes you (the children) feel good about yourself (themselves)?" and "What do I do that hurts your (the children's) feelings?"

Third, ask yourself what impact you think your relationship with your own parents has had on your ability to love your spouse and children. To what degree did you feel loved, valued, and respected when you were a child? How were you disciplined? Did you feel understood? Complete the survey, "How Did My Parents Meet My Childhood Needs?" Fourth, complete the survey, "How Well Do I Think My Heavenly Father Meets My Needs?" Once you identify distorted concepts of love and the relational patterns upon which they are based, you can seek God for help. He will want to show you through His Word and through the counsel of others His way of demonstrating discipline, comfort, protection, and guidance.

Paul tells us in Romans that we no longer need to be enslaved by patterns of thought we may have acquired in childhood. Through the help of the Holy Spirit, who communicates the truth of God's Word to us, our heavenly Father can renew our corrupt beliefs about love, as well as the impaired relational patterns we have with Him and others as a result.

Do not conform any longer to the pattern of this world, but be transformed by the renewing of your mind. (Romans 12:2)

As you identify patterns of thought that limit your ability to love your spouse and children, ask God to forgive you. Renounce any wrong ideas or behaviors that fail to meet their emotional needs and communicate true love. Then allow God to show you the truth about His love. Ask Him to reveal His love to you so that it is real to your heart.

Meeting Needs Evaluation Surveys

How Am I Meeting My Children's Needs?
(Personal Survey)
Rate yourself on a scale of 1–10
(1 = very rarely, 10 = always)

[   ] I demonstrate unconditional acceptance
[   ] I show affirmation and approval
[   ] I show affection in respectful ways
[   ] I acknowledge my children's thoughts and feelings
[   ] I am quick to forgive
[   ] I discipline calmly
[   ] I consistently enforce limits
[   ] I offer guidance for living
[   ] I listen with intent to understand
[   ] I am aware of my children's needs

How Does My Family Feel I Am Meeting Their Needs?
(Feedback from Family Members)
Rate _____ on a scale of 1–10
(1 = very rarely, 10 = always)

[   ] _____ demonstrates unconditional acceptance
[   ] _____ shows affirmation and approval
[   ] _____ shows affection in respectful ways
[   ] _____ acknowledges other people's thoughts and feelings
[   ] _____ is quick to forgive
[   ] _____ disciplines calmly
[   ] _____ consistently enforces limits
[   ] _____ offers guidance for living
[   ] _____ listens with intent to understand
[   ] _____ is aware of other people's needs

Meeting Needs Evaluation Surveys

How Did My Parents Meet My Childhood Needs?

Rate your father/mother on a scale of 1–10
(1 = very rarely, 10 = always)

Father Mother

[   ]   [   ] Demonstrated unconditional acceptance
[   ]   [   ] Showed affirmation and approval
[   ]   [   ] Showed affection in respectful ways
[   ]   [   ] Acknowledged my thoughts and feelings
[   ]   [   ] Was quick to forgive
[   ]   [   ] Disciplined calmly
[   ]   [   ] Consistently enforced limits
[   ]   [   ] Offered guidance for living
[   ]   [   ] Listened with intent to understand
[   ]   [   ] Was aware of my needs

How Well Do I Think My Heavenly Father Meets My Needs?

Rate Your Perception of God's Care on a Scale of 1–10
(1 = very rarely, 10 = always)

[   ] Demonstrates unconditional acceptance
[   ] Shows affirmation and approval
[   ] Shows affection in respectful ways
[   ] Acknowledges my thoughts and feelings
[   ] Is quick to forgive
[   ] Disciplines calmly
[   ] Consistently enforces limits
[   ] Offers guidance for living
[   ] Listens with intent to understand
[   ] Is aware of my needs

Service Projects and Chart

I s a chore by any other name still a chore? Not necessarily. Children tend to think of "chores" as "helping Mom out before she blows a fuse." Performing chores for no greater reason than to stave off a parent's wrath tends to sap motivation by undermining a freedom to contribute to the well-being of the family.

So how do we encourage our family members to take personal responsibility for making their beds, doing the dishes, and changing the cat litter? We begin by changing the way we think about and refer to these household tasks. It is better to think and speak of tasks around the house as "family service projects" so that all family members cultivate a willingness to serve and a sense of ownership for the condition of the home.

Instead of saying, "Tommy, the cat litter stinks! Do your chores," try "Tommy, if you don't take care of the litter, the whole house will smell." Rather than, "I need you to set the table now," say, "We are counting on you to set the table so we can eat."

What about "allowances" or paying children to perform family service projects? If work around the house is part of what it means to be a family member, should children expect to be paid? The question is not whether parents should pay for their children's service around the house (I think that's fine), but rather who is perceived to own the work around the house and take responsibility for its condition? Does Mom hire her children to work since she can't do it all? If this is her motivation, then the kids are likely to protest their labor conditions and strike for higher wages. In reality, what we call chores are really duties—work that belongs to everyone.

Instead of "Chore Charts," think in terms of "Service Projects" and give kids the chance to contribute to the well-being of their family through heartfelt service. Remember to inspect (and reward) the projects you expect of your child as recorded on the Service Project Chart. Look for attitude more than perfection in the performance of a job, since children mature at their own paces and not all kids are capable of advanced chores at the same age.

Service Projects 2- and 3-Year-Olds Can Do
- Hang up clothes on hangers
- Help make the bed
- Pick up toys and books
- Take laundry to the laundry room
- Help feed pets
- Help wipe up messes
- Dust, using socks on their hands
- Mop certain areas, with help

Service Projects 4- and 5-Year-Olds Can Do (in addition to the above)
- Set and clear the table
- Dust
- Sweep the floor
- Make beds
- Some cooking and meal preparation
- Put away groceries

Service Projects for Ages 6-8 (in addition to the above)
- Take out trash
- Fold and put away laundry
- Take care of pets
- Vacuum and mop

Service Projects for Ages 9-12 (in addition to the above)
- Clean the bathroom
- Clean and wash the car
- Rake leaves
- Weed gardens
- Operate the washer and dryer
- Make simple breakfasts and lunches
- Wash dishes

Service Projects for Ages 13-17 (in addition to the above)
- Clean out garage
- Change air-conditioning and water filters
- Mow lawn
- Clean inside of refrigerator and other kitchen appliances
- Minor car maintenance—oil and tire checks
- Prepare grocery lists
- Prepare meals
- Replace light bulbs and vacuum cleaner bags
- All parts of the laundry
- Wash windows

Sample Chart (Make One for Each Child)

In service to my family:	Sun	Mon	Tue	Wed	Thu	Fri	Sat
Make bed							
Set table							
Wash dishes							
Empty trash							
Feed dog							

Discipline Checklist

Questions to Ask Yourself

- Am I focused on correcting the behavior or venting frustration?
- Is my goal to teach my child or to just punish/get even?
- Am I able to speak respectfully when I correct my child?
- What would I look like if saw myself through my child's eyes right now?
- Does the consequence fit the infraction?
- Are the consequences for wrong behavior natural? (For example, if your child writes on the wall, the punishment should be to clean it off.)

Discipline Checklist

[ ] I will discipline as soon as possible so that my child associates the misbehavior with its consequence.

[ ] For my younger child, a time-out is my first line of defense.

[ ] For my older children, I will use agreements in writing for expected behavior and discipline.

[ ] I will be firm, fair, and consistent.

[ ] I will work with my spouse to make sure we both agree on the discipline and follow through.

[   ] I (and my spouse) will decide which behaviors must be dealt with firmly and which can be handled in a more flexible manner. I will choose my battles wisely.

[   ] If I can't agree with my spouse, we will agree to seek advice from someone we both respect.

[   ] I will try to give my children as much responsibility and choice as they can handle without physical injury.

[   ] I will reward good behavior with praise in order to encourage my child to continue the behavior. (See list of praise and encouraging statements, below.)

PRAISE AND ENCOURAGING STATEMENTS

• Exceptional • Fantastic Work! • Breathtaking! • Awesome!
• You're a Great Example for Others! • Keep Up the Good Work
• I Knew You Had It in You! • You Should Be Proud!
• What an Imagination! •You're Sensational • Good for You
• Very Good! • Take a Bow • Super Job • How Thoughtful of You
• Nice Going! • Well Done • You're Inspiring • How Artistic!
• You Go the Extra Mile • Hooray for You • You're a Joy
• You're a Shining Star • You're Amazing • What A Great Idea!
• You're Getting Better • You're Tops • You Figured It Out
• You Blow Me Away! • You're #1 • Remarkable! • You're a Winner!
• Beautiful! • High Five! • Wow! • Magnificent! • You're A-OK
• You've Made Progress! • Brilliant! • Thanks for Helping
• Thanks for Caring • Great Discovery • What a Genius!
• You're Very Talented • How Original • Congratulations!
• You're a Champ • You're Super! • I'm Impressed • You're the Greatest
• I'm Proud of You • The Time You Put in Really Shows! • Bravo!
• That's Incredible • Great! • Clever • Outstanding Performance
• Wonderful! • Amazing Effort! • Unbelievable Work • Phenomenal!
• You've Got It • Superb! • You're Special • Cool! • Excellent!
• Way to Go! • You've Outdone Yourself • Thumbs Up • Fabulous!
• What a Great Listener • Your Help Counts! • You Made It Happen!
• Terrific! • You're So Cool • It Couldn't Be Better!
• You Have What It Takes!

Rules of Our House:

WRITING A FAMILY COVENANT

This appendix provides a method for introducing and communicating expectations for behavior in a way that encourages compliance, the development of good judgment, and family fun.

In a relaxed family meeting (complete with snacks), create a code of conduct with input from every family member. Each participant is asked to recommend rules that encourage personal safety, kindness, and respect for personal property. These rules are written down, discussed, and amended. When there is consensus, they are written down in final form and placed in a visible location like a refrigerator door. Some families choose to decorate their family covenant with a self-designed family coat of arms.

It has been my experience that when children are asked to help write the rules of their home, they are more demanding than their parents would be of their behavior—even as teens. (Parents have veto power, but are advised to use it sparingly.)

The following page provides a sample format that you may want to use in writing your family covenant.

We pledge to follow the Rules of Our House,

The _____ Family Covenant

- We will show our loyalty to God by:

- We will respect each other's feelings by:

- We will respect each other's property by:

- In taking care of our house, we will:

- When we hurt someone's feelings, we will:

- When we hurt someone, we will:

- When we are corrected, we will:

- When others come over to the house, we will:

- When we get frustrated, we will:

- To honor our parents/children, we will:

Family Communication Agreement

U se this chart to form a "contract" between you and your child. A Family Communication Agreement helps reduce the potential for conflict by clarifying expectations, providing accountability, and establishing voluntary agreement to meet specific objectives for behavior. These goals may pertain to homework, school performance, curfews, car use, pet care, and even dating.

> **Instructions:** Parent and child write out their mutually shared goal. Example: "For Bobby to get his homework done without Mom nagging." Parent and child then write out what they need and expect from one another to fulfill their goal. Example from child: "I need Mom to remind me only once." Example from parent: "I need Bobby to be finished by 10 p.m." Make sure to copy the agreement for each participant of the contract.

Below are examples of mutually shared goals, followed by examples of needs and expectations that might appear in the section "What I Need from You":

Mutually Shared Goals
- To speak respectfully to each other
- To respect each other's privacy
- To be on time for things
- To have a clean home
- To have a warm dinner
- To get along peacefully
- To have personal privacy

- To not worry when the other person is out late
- To have a fun and friendly family

To meet a mutually shared goal, a parent might need a child to:

- Ask permission before you take things.
- Put things back where they belong.
- Call and let us know if you will be late.
- Be honest so that I can trust you.
- Listen to me.
- Don't complain.
- Admit when you are wrong ("I'm sorry").
- Don't wait until the last minute to ask for help.

To meet a mutually shared goal, a child might request a parent to:

- Listen to me and don't jump to conclusions.
- Give me a chance to prove myself.
- Respect what I have to say.
- Don't judge me until you've heard me.
- Don't nag me.
- Don't be grumpy.
- Admit when you are wrong ("I'm sorry").
- Knock before you enter my room.

Communication Agreement between

_____ and _____

Goal: _____

What I Need from You	**What You Need from Me**
• _____	• _____
• _____	• _____
• _____	• _____
• _____	• _____
• _____	• _____
• _____	• _____

Raising "Fear-less" Kids in a Frightening World

HELPING CHILDREN TO TRUST GOD AND OVERCOME FEAR

On September 11, 2001, my twelve-year-old daughter came home from school, like many other children, in need of answers, comfort, and reassurance. "Dad," she said in an unusually serious tone, "is this the tribulation?" I've taught kids the Bible for twenty years, and I've never had to field a tougher question! Rachael was looking for more than Bible facts; she wanted to hear something that would sooth her fears. After I regained my composure, I put my arm around her and whispered, "Rach, some pretty scary things have happened today, haven't they? What it all means, I'm not sure. But I do know that God is right here with us now and that we will be okay." With that, she skipped carefree up to her room. I exhaled a quiet prayer, "Thanks, God."

The world has changed. A large commercial jet flew low over an intersection where I waited for a light a few months ago. The person in the car next to me unrolled his window and strained to watch the plane fly out of sight. I knew what he was thinking. As I looked in the rearview mirror and saw my children sitting quietly in the backseat, I wondered what kind of future awaited them. Safety at schools, on the streets, and in airports is unlikely to be taken for granted for years to come. How do we prepare our children for such a frightening world? First, we must cultivate a healthy capacity for trust in our children, through which they may access resources greater than their own. Hopefully, this includes our guidance and emotional support. Second, we must help them to gain strategies for overcoming fear—strategies that are honed from learning to manage fears faced on a daily basis. Children who know how to overcome the fear of ridicule, rejection, math exams, and gym teachers are outfitted for adult-sized anxieties. Below are six principles for training children to confront fear.

1. Cultivate in your children a healthy capacity to trust.

2. Help your children to identify their feelings.

3. Help your children to identify the underlying reason(s) for fear.

4. Allow them to come up with their own plan for handling fear. (Kids don't rebel against their own solutions.)

5. Model trust in God during times of uncertainty and fear.

6. Control the flow of fear-provoking information.

1. CULTIVATE A HEALTHY CAPACITY TO TRUST.

It's impossible for children to draw upon your strength, receive comfort, and take your advice if they are not convinced that you have their best interests in mind. Trust is like a spiritual umbilical cord. It allows nourishing emotional resources to pass back and forth between two souls. When trust is damaged, it leaves a child to fend for himself. A child who is continually disappointed or hurt by a parent develops self-protective and self-reliant means of managing his needs—patterns of behavior that seek to handle fear in one's own strength and that are characterized by pride, anger, and rebellion.

Children who grow up in warm, stable, and loving environments where it is safe to be honest about their feelings and needs, and where trust is reinforced, learn the reasonableness of placing trust and faith in others to meet their needs. Vulnerability and honesty are seen as acceptable risks. A healthy capacity to trust is, in fact, the emotional groundwork of faith—affording an individual the ability to freely give himself away to God.

How can we cultivate our children's ability to trust? Showing respect and understanding for their feelings is probably the most effective way parents can build trust and earn their children's confidence. For example, when your child is feeling afraid, honor her feelings rather than trying to change them. Say, "Honey, a lot of people feel afraid when they face a bully," rather than "Listen girl, you gotta be tough in this world!" Or, when word-problem anxiety strikes, instead of saying, "Come on, it's not that hard. You just need to concentrate more!" say, "That's a tough problem for you. But I've seen you master hard problems before. What can I do to help?"

Sometimes Christian parents, in an effort to encourage their children, unintentionally minimize their feelings with well-meaning platitudes. "Honey, don't be afraid…just trust God." Banishing feelings (even for the cause of greater faith) will not make them vanish—it only drives them underground. For teens, cultivating trust means we convince them that we share their goals for independence and competence in the world. This means we look for more ways to say yes than to say no and to give them as much freedom as they can handle responsibly.

2. HELP YOUR CHILDREN TO IDENTIFY THEIR FEELINGS.

Helping your children to acknowledge their fears is the first step in overcoming them. Sometimes just naming the emotion brings relief. When a child is able to admit, "Daddy, I feel afraid," he feels less helpless and out of control.

Ask open-ended questions to help your child understand his feelings: "What's going on? What are you feeling?" Be careful not to ask questions that accuse. Questions like, "Why did you say that?" and "Why are you acting this way?" cause children to hide their feelings. Second, speculate on their feelings: "Are you afraid? A lot of children feel afraid when they see such scary pictures and hear such scary things on TV."

3. HELP YOUR CHILDREN TO IDENTIFY THE UNDERLYING REASON(S) FOR THEIR FEARS.

In order to overcome fear, we must identify and disarm the underlying belief that sustains it. Ridicule, for instance, is most painful for children who have underlying doubts about themselves. If a child believes he is ugly or stupid, he is more likely to take the teasing of his friends personally. The ten-year-old boy who is afraid of being called "dumb" by his peers at school, for instance, may suffer from the belief that what his friends say may indeed be true. By helping kids realize the truth about themselves or the facts about a particular event, we remove fear's teeth.

Example: My six-year-old was watching the evening news the day of the attack on America and saw footage of the destruction of the World Trade Center from that morning. Suddenly, she began to cry, "Oh no! Another plane crash into a building!" Each time she saw the replay of the horrific event, my poor daughter believed it was another plane crash. Accurately interpreting frightening information to which our children are exposed reduces fear and anxiety. "The truth will set them free!"

The Bible indicates that to overcome fear, we must destroy *"speculations and every lofty thing raised up against the knowledge of God"* and take *"every thought captive to the obedience of Christ"* (2 Corinthians 10:5 NASB). Note that Scripture says we are to take every thought captive—not every emotion. Fear cannot be converted, renewed, or transformed. The beliefs that underlie and fuel the emotion, thoughts that contradict the knowledge of God, however, can be taken captive and replaced with the truth. We might ask the ten-year-old who fears the ridicule of his peers, "Does God think you are dumb? What does Psalm 139:14 say? How do I feel about you? Do you believe me?"

Help your children get the facts. The facts about who they are, who God is, and how real the threat of loss really is.

In our zeal to correct our children's thinking, we must not neglect their profound need to be understood. Kids feel violated if advice is given before their feelings are acknowledged and understood. If an eight-year-old boy whose parents are getting a divorce worries about who will care for him, rather than saying, "Don't worry. God says all things work together for good," bring comfort by acknowledging his fear. "Josh, a lot of boys your age feel alone and wonder if anyone will take care of them when their parents go through a divorce." Understanding brings healing to hurting emotions.

4. Let children come up with their own plan for handling fear.

Kids rebel against our ideas, not their own! When children, especially teens, feel like we are limiting their opportunities to gain independence and to think for themselves, they are likely to resist us. That's why wise parents encourage their children to come up with their own solutions to fearful situations. Example: Rather than our saying, "Don't worry about the math final. I'll show you what you have to know," to which the child huffs and puffs impatiently, say, "Math final, that's rough. I'm here if you need me."

In our zeal to bring comfort and reassurance, we can often do more harm than good. Moms and dads who allow their parental instincts to run amuck solve all their children's problems and handle all their fears. "I can't believe those rotten kids called you 'dumb.' I'm going to call your teacher right now! No one gets away with calling my child names!" Unintentionally, an "overprotective" parent robs her child of opportunities to hone problem-solving skills, learn strategies for overcoming fear, and grow in confidence. Children whose parents "take care" of their fears not only grow up ill prepared for the real world, but also grow up believing that something must be wrong with them since they were never allowed to take care of themselves.

To foster confidence and problem solving in her child, a mother might try responding with, "Being called a name hurts. What can you do to stop it?" And rather than offering unsolicited advice, she might ask, "Would you like to know what I do when someone says something mean about me?" By asking permission, rather than dictating what her child should do, she helps her to feel that her decision-making counts.

When kids are younger (preschool age), a great way to handle fear is to play! One mother frantically shared with me, the week after September 11, "I think there is something wrong with my son. He keeps building Lego towers and crashing his toy plane into them." She was relieved to discover that this was totally normal. Children often act out their fears in play. Instead of reacting negatively to behavior that seems violent or horrific, play with the child. "Let's get the fire trucks and save those people in the building. We need to pray for them." Playing with our children during times of stress is God's therapy for kids. Encourage your child to write a story, draw a picture, or act out the fear-provoking event in order to help him resolve his anxiety.

5. MODEL TRUST IN GOD DURING TIMES OF UNCERTAINTY AND FEAR.

This is a hard one—especially if you are struggling with fear yourself. As long as you are not so emotionally overwhelmed that you lose your objectivity, it is a good idea to discuss your battle against fear with your children. By doing so, you can offer an example of how to manage anxiety. "I'm scared too, honey, but I know that God is with us and can help us, and that makes me feel better. What do you say we pray about it?"

If you are overtaken by fear and unable to help your children cope, give your children the opportunity to talk with someone who can offer support and help them problem-solve with God's guidance.

6. CONTROL THE FLOW OF FEAR-PROVOKING INFORMATION.

Many baby boomers recall the looming fear of nuclear war that hung over them when they were children. I remember, as a child, for instance, lying awake in bed thinking that it would be better to die from the initial blast than to die slowly from radiation poisoning. Sick, I know, but I bet I have friends out there who thought the same thing! Information can be a heavy burden for children. It is extremely important to keep exposure to frightening news coverage, movies, and video games to a minimum—especially when kids are small. By controlling the flow of media into our homes and accurately interpreting the data that children see and hear, parents can reduce the level of anxiety in their children. One parent, on September 11, calmed the fears of his nine-year-old boy by asking, "How far away is New York City? Do terrible things like this happen every day? How can we pray for those people?"

Though we cannot always prevent fearful events from entering into our children's lives, we can help them to develop lifelong strategies for coping with fear—methods that spark faith and deepen their dependency on God. A "fear-less" child may still get scared, but, properly trained, he has the means to disarm the underlying beliefs that sustain the emotion and to encourage himself with his faith in God.

The single most effective weapon our children have to overcome anxiety, fear, and stress is trust in God. Fear is the absence of trust in God's availability, goodness, and power. It is always based upon a lie that seeks to make God out to be less than who He really is. Where there is true knowledge of God and complete dependency upon His love and strength, fear cannot exist. By reinforcing our children's capacity to trust, exposing the false beliefs that fuel their fears, providing them with the facts about who God really is, and providing an example of what it means to depend on God, we prepare our kids to live fearlessly in a frightening world.

Decision-Making Matrix

Teach your children to make wise choices by using a decision-making matrix. The matrix provides a child with an opportunity to think through the consequences of his actions by breaking down a desired outcome into identifiable choices.

A child, and especially a teen, is far less resistant to support and guidance when a parent ventures to problem-solve with the child and encourage him to think for himself. To help avoid power struggles with your child, make the decision-making matrix a part of granting approval to new freedoms and choices. No doubt, your child will be motivated to use the matrix if a new freedom is at stake!

Each question outlined in the flowchart on the next page is designed to help your child foresee the consequences of his choices. The matrix is extremely helpful in teaching a child the value of delayed gratification.

You may want to reread pages 139–141 to review the purpose and parameters of the Decision-Making Matrix. Remember that giving your child choices does not mean that you give up parental control and protection. As a general rule, we should permit a child only as much freedom as he or she can handle responsibly.

Decision-Making Matrix

Begin by explaining to your child that sometimes things that feel good at first can feel really bad later because of their consequences. And sometimes things that feel bad at first can feel great later because of their results.

Ask child: What do you want to do? _____

Explore the Consequences
A. If you make this choice, what might happen that would make you feel good? What might happen that would make you feel bad?

A1. I might feel good because:

_____

A2. I might feel bad because:

_____

Ask child: If you made this choice and felt bad, what other choice could you make to change the bad feelings? _____

Explore the Consequences
B. What may happen as a result of your choice that would make you feel good? What may happen to make you feel bad?

B1. I might feel good because:

_____

B2. I might feel bad because:

_____

Ask child: What choice could you make to change the bad feelings? _____

Explore the Consequences
C. What may happen as a result of your choice that would make you feel good? What could make you feel bad?

C1. I might feel good because:

_____

C2. I might feel bad because:

_____

Becoming a Parent of Destiny Checklist

CHECKLIST FOR *RAISING CHILDREN ON PURPOSE*

_____1. I am able to identify the gifting and passion of my child.

_____2. I provide classroom education and practical experience that develop my child's gifting and feed his/her passion.

_____3. I meet my child's seven emotional needs:

_____Protection

_____Acceptance

_____Recognition

_____Enforced Limits

_____Nearness

_____Time

_____Support

_____4. I introduce my child to Christ.

_____5. I pray daily for my child's calling to be fulfilled.

About the Author
and His Ministry

Wesley H. Fleming is founder and director of Coming Home Ministries, a curriculum and conferencing ministry to parents and Christian educators that purposes to strengthen the bond between church and home and help parents become their children's primary spiritual influence. He has worked in the field of Christian education for twenty-five years as a pastor and ministers extensively in parent and teacher training. He has been published in *Family Times, Parenting Today, Vision New England,* and *Children's Ministry Magazine.* He is currently the pastor of Eastside Vineyard Church in New York State. Mr. Fleming is married and has three children.

Coming Home Ministries
3618 Pompey Center Road
Manlius, NY 13104
Website: http://www.cominghomeministries.com

On the following pages are Coming Home Ministries' parenting seminars and Christian education workshops.

Parenting Seminars for Churches and Regional Conferences

Raising Children on Purpose Seminar (Saturday Seminar)

You can know the "way" your children are to go—their God-given purpose in life—through an easy-to-use gift and spiritual passion survey tool called the DNA (Divine Notion Awaiting) Analysis. Also, learn how to encourage children to stay on their "way" by helping them to develop a healthy capacity to trust, an accurate perception of God, and to maintain a personal relationship with Christ. Adapted from the book *Raising Children on Purpose* by Wesley Fleming.

The Seven Destiny Makers—Seven Things Kids Need to Succeed (Saturday Seminar)

Discover seven qualities that assure a child success in any field and learn how to impart them. Children need a well-nourished soul, a hunger for God, a capacity to love, self-discipline, good judgment, a teachable spirit, and a sense of purpose to achieve their destinies. Adapted from the book *The Seven Destiny Makers.*

I'm Hungry, Mom! What's for Dinner? (Saturday Seminar)

We give away what we have—for better or for worse. To give our children the love they need, we must receive it first. Truth: Many of us have little to give, and our families are going "hungry" because we were never spiritually well nourished by our own parents. Your Father in heaven offers you the opportunity to be born into the arms of a perfect Parent and to be re-parented in His perfect love. Break the cycle. Identify and remove barriers you have in trusting God as your Father, fill your plate with His love, and begin to serve your family from a full plate.

CHRISTIAN EDUCATION WORKSHOPS FOR CHURCHES AND REGIONAL CONFERENCES

Combine all three workshops for a full day of inspirational teacher training. Customize workshops to your needs. Need a fun event for Teacher Award night? Check out "Oh, no. Tomorrow is Sunday!" on the website.

Snore No More (Two-hour workshop)

Eliminate Boredom Forever in your children's church and Sunday School classes. This high-powered, hands-on, teacher-training workshop presents the three keys to a dynamic educational experience: Experience, Belonging, and Fun. Get them off the back row and on the edge of their seats. Learn to teach in such a way that kids (and adults) learn and love it.

Divine Appointment—Recruiting in the New Millennium (Two-hour workshop)

Trouble finding workers? Need an assistant? Develop a recruiting program that lets the Lord of the Harvest be your "Head Hunter." No more round pegs in square holes; God has a better way. Discover heavenly yet practical principles for communicating your church's needs, finding the right people, and keeping them. The workers are there—let Him show you.

Why Johnny Can't Sit Down (Two-hour workshop)

Reduce problem behavior greatly by learning to work with the wiggle, not against it! Effectively manage your classroom by clearly communicating your expectations, setting realistic limits, and applying appropriate awards and consequences. Prevent unwanted distractions by teaching in the way kids like to learn. Plus: what to do about troubled kids. Help them to listen—and to like it!